# The Complete Guide to Query Letters for Travel Writers

ROY STEVENSON

Copyright © 2016 Nomadic Publishing LLC

All rights reserved.

ISBN-10:1537522132
ISBN-13: 978-1537522135

## DISCLAIMER:

The information and recommendations contained in this manual have been compiled from sources considered to be reliable. Use of the information and recommendations contained herein is at the discretion and sole responsibility of the reader. The travel industry is in a constant state of flux and everything in these pages is subject to change. All attempts have been made to ensure information was correct at the time of writing, but it's important to verify all information yourself. This publication is designed to provide accurate and authoritative information in regard to the subject matter covered based on the author's experience. There are no guarantees that your experience will be the same. It is sold and distributed with the understanding that Nomadic Publishing LLC, the author, affiliates, editor, designer, publisher or seller are not engaged in rendering legal, accounting, or any other professional advice or service. If legal or other expert assistance is required, the services of a competent professional advisor should be sought.

# CONTENTS

**INTRODUCTION** ............................................................................................................ 6
My Story and Why I Wrote This Book ........................................................................ 6

**HOW TO SELL YOUR TRAVEL STORIES** ........................................................................ 9
Why You Need Query Letters ..................................................................................... 9
How To Make Your Query Letters Resonate With Editors ...................................... 12
After the Query Letter ............................................................................................... 24
Query Letter Format and Sequence ......................................................................... 27
Getting Paid ................................................................................................................ 29

**TWENTY SAMPLE QUERY LETTERS** ............................................................................ 30
A Fascinating Day Trip: Regional Magazine ............................................................. 33
An Unusual Story Angle: Niche Magazine ................................................................ 36
Sell Your Story Internationally: Specialty Magazine ................................................ 39
Use Active Verbs: Inflight Magazine ......................................................................... 42
Breaking into a New Genre: Art Magazine ............................................................... 45
New Writer, Few Credentials: Specialty Magazine .................................................. 49
Paint Pictures: Words & Photos: Adventure Magazine ........................................... 53
Describe Your Readers: International Travel Magazine .......................................... 57
Research Before You Query: Specialty Magazine .................................................... 61
Break the Rules: International Travel Magazine ...................................................... 65
Build Repeat Business: Top Shelf History Magazine ................................................ 70
Make the Editor Salivate: Beer Magazine ................................................................ 74
Co-Authoring and Intrigue: Beer Magazine ............................................................. 78
Show Your Enthusiasm: Automobile Magazine ....................................................... 82
Build Long-Term Relationships: Military Magazine ................................................. 85
"Dear Editor" Query: Specialty Magazine ................................................................ 89
Repackaging and Repurposing Your Stories: Yachting Magazine ........................... 93
Use Available Content in Your Query: Cruise Magazine ......................................... 97
Provide High Quality Photos: Military Magazine ................................................... 100
Tweaking Your Template: Top Shelf Magazine ...................................................... 103

**BEYOND THE QUERY LETTER** ................................................................................... 107
Marketing Mastery Formula™ ................................................................................ 107

**WRITER'S RESOURCES** ............................................................................................. 109

**ABOUT THE AUTHOR** ............................................................................................... 111

# INTRODUCTION

## MY STORY AND WHY I WROTE THIS BOOK

I started freelance writing in 2007, after attending a three-day travel writing workshop. Since then I've had 800 articles published in 190 different magazines, newspapers, websites, in-flights and on-boards. I have a stack of magazines and newspapers six feet high to prove these claims.

Within three months of starting freelance writing, my stories began appearing on the national magazine racks without interruption. When I go to my local and big chain bookstores, I can always find several magazines with my articles in them. My work has appeared in magazines and newspapers in the United States, Canada, England, Scotland, Ireland, Australia, New Zealand and South Africa.

I've had more than thirty cover feature stories. I contribute regularly to more than a dozen magazines and speak at writer's conferences around the U.S. I've been featured in *The Writer* and *Writer's News* magazines, and I write for several writing magazines and websites about the keys to my success.

I have yet to hear of any other freelance writer who has approached this sort of productivity, although there must be others out there. There have been times when I've had as many as 32 articles stacked up to write, and these days I seldom have fewer than ten assignments on my desk. It is not unusual for editors to email me asking if I will write something for them, and fast.

It was only in 2009, when I attended a travel writer's conference that I realized how quickly I had advanced in the freelance writing game in such a short time. This revelation came to me when a professional travel writer on a panel, told us how proud she was to have been published in 100 magazines in ten years.

I remember thinking, "Ten years? What's the big deal? It took me only 25 months to do that."

Then, in discussions with other veteran freelance writers at conferences, several were astonished to learn that I'd had such a prolific number of bylines in such a short time.

You might be thinking that my writing success is all because I'm a superb writer. The fact is, my writing is good, maybe above average, but definitely not fine prose.

I don't have a degree in creative writing. Nor do I have a market on great story ideas. I don't teach writing at an Ivy League University.

In fact, my graduate degree is in a field completely unrelated to writing. I started out as a physical education teacher - definitely not a professional group known for its writing. Then I studied to be an exercise physiologist. I taught exercise science at the community college and university level for many years.

Yet, despite my humble writing credentials, I'm clearly doing something right.

Most freelancers are pleased with a 10% to 20% acceptance rate for their stories. When I pitch a story idea I know there is a 90% chance it will be picked up for publication in a magazine or two somewhere around the world.

I'm not writing of these successes to feed my own ego or to brag about my success. The reason I'm telling you my story is so you know that:

**If you want to write and get published successfully, and if you have average writing ability, you can sell your articles to dozens, even hundreds, of print and online publications.**

I'm a teacher at heart, so I want to teach other people how to do the things I've done. I've published a detailed marketing manual with my entire sales process explaining how I do what I do. (You can find more information about my other books in the Writer's Resources at the end of this book.)

*The Complete Guide to Query Letters for Travel Writers,* is about one critical aspect of marketing - your query letter. It's your first step to understanding how to successfully get published.

So let's get started…

---

**Note:** Throughout this book are links to my website created especially for travel writers, www.PitchTravelWrite.com. Because this is a print book, you obviously won't be able to click on the links. But I've shown them in blue as a hyperlink to make them easier to find. (You can purchase the Kindle version or the PDF version if you want the capability to click on the links.)

Type the URL into your search engine window to go directly to the page on www.PitchTravelWrite.com. This will give you more detail on that topic. These topics are related content, but beyond the scope of this book.

# HOW TO SELL YOUR TRAVEL STORIES

## WHY YOU NEED QUERY LETTERS

A Query letter pitches your story idea to an editor and requests the opportunity to write the story for them.

Query letters used to be mailed to editors (with a stamp and envelope). These days, the vast majority are sent by email.

When you're starting out in freelance writing, a full, detailed query letter is a requirement. The query letter explains your idea enough to intrigue the editor, and points out where the story might fit into the magazine.

Your query letter shows the editor that you've thought the story through and gives you a chance to show your writing skills. This is your sales pitch. Then you back up your pitch by demonstrating that you can be trusted to write a good story and deliver it on time by showing your credentials.

Your query letter is framed to offer a coherent and concrete idea that matches the magazine's content. And, you want to convince the editor that you're the right person to write the story.

That's a lot to expect in one or two pages!

Eventually, as you become more established as a writer and build your bylines, editors will get to know you. Some will call you and assign stories. Some will be willing to take shorter pitches, and you won't have to work as hard at selling your story ideas.

But that's later. Starting out, just thing of a query letter as your sales tool.

One of the most asked questions about query letters is:

*"Can I send the editor my completed article instead of writing a query letter?"*

I hear this question from many aspiring writers. They believe that you go on a trip, then come home and write a story about it. Then, you send the story off to a magazine or newspaper editor who magically accepts it, and publishes it a few days later.

**This doesn't happen.**

The reality of travel writing is quite different. Writing an article before selling it to an editor is a formula for disappointment. This is a classic beginner's mistake.

And that's where the query letter enters the picture. A query letter is your sales tool. It helps you get your story idea accepted before you book your airfare, take the trip, or write the article.

Selling your article before you write it saves time for everyone involved in the process. Most importantly, you won't waste time writing an article that no one wants. Write your query letter before you write your story. (http://www.pitchtravelwrite.com/sales-pitch.html)

Think about it. What happens if you spend a few days writing your article, and then no one is interested in buying it? You've wasted your time, and you'll feel rejected.

**The generally accepted and much easier approach is to write the query first.**

After you've written a few dozen query letters, you'll find that it doesn't take long to crank them out. If you have all your research materials handy it can take you as little as 15 minutes to write one. Some may take longer if they require a great deal of research.

Often I send out the same query letter to ten or fifteen magazines at the same time. Known as simultaneous submissions, it still only takes me another half hour to do this. This is a much shorter time commitment than writing a whole story.

A query letter also gives the editor a chance to see your idea and recommend any changes that he or she would like to see when you actually submit the story later on.

Then, with feedback from the editor, you can fit your article perfectly to the magazine. Perhaps the editor would like your story to be longer or shorter than you suggest. Or, maybe he wants some interviews or a focus on a different aspect of your story.

Occasionally, an editor might suggest an entirely different topic about your destination. Since you haven't written the story yet, this isn't a problem. You can do it.

So always query first, before you write your story. This will save you so much time and heartbreak later on.

I also believe in writing query letters and getting assignments before you take the trip. (http://www.pitchtravelwrite.com/presell.html) There are many reasons for this, and I've elaborated on this topic on my website.

Not everyone does this. But, for me, it's the most proactive approach to travel writing. Have a look the article on my website if you want to understand more about why it's best to do it this way.

# HOW TO MAKE YOUR QUERY LETTERS RESONATE WITH EDITORS

I've made a serious study of marketing techniques and query letters since I started freelance writing. I've lived and breathed sales techniques in order to get my stories out into the world.

After many years of experimentation, I've learned what works in a query letter to an editor, and what doesn't work. By adding and tweaking my query letters over the past several years, I've developed a nice format that seems to work for most magazines.

My own query letters have intentionally become quite formulaic. I don't individually craft every word anymore. Instead, I use a template and then tweak the template for each story. Doing it this way saves time, and it works. That, after all, is the most important measure of our success.

Before we get to the sample query letters that have worked for me, there are certain elements to discuss. I consider these essential elements because they are all pieces that form a successful query. None of them are difficult or complex. What's important is that you keep them in mind and include them when you're drafting your query letters.

The next several pages describes the essential elements needed in a successful query letter.

## Have a catchy title and strong opener.

Your opening must catch the editor's attention. Ask yourself, if the editor only reads the first three or four sentences of my query, will it capture their interest?

If your opener doesn't sound exciting, improve it. It must be intriguing or enticing in some way.

There are numerous techniques that travel writer's use to jazz up their query opener. They range from offering a problem and solution to providing valuable information. Some travel writers use a question in their opener to pique the editor's attention. Braver writers use a personal anecdote as an opener.

Here's an example of using a question for your opener: "Are you interested in giving your readers a unique insight into Prague's lesser known attractions that only the locals know about?"

Dream up a catchy title for your story.

A short title that captures the essence of your story works best. But, there are other times you just have to state the title as if it was news on the electronic reader board in Times Square.

After I finished a nice little story about eagle watching on the Nooksack River, the title I submitted was pretty mundane: "Eagles Gathering on the Nooksack River are One of Washington's Most Spectacular Natural Sights". Well, at least there's no way that title leaves any room for misinterpretation!

Short and catchy is best, but don't stress over the title. In most cases the editor will change it anyway.

## Know your slant.

It's not enough to tell an editor that you want to write a story about Paris, or Berlin, or your favorite place. You need a specific slant or angle.

Every travel magazine has published a general roundup story about Paris, and these days the editors want to know about the unique, unknown aspects of Paris that haven't been discovered. Editors will toss out vague, non-specific story ideas immediately. Before submitting a story idea, always ask yourself "what is different about this story that will entice an editor and command the attention of a reader?"

## Keep your query short: 1-2 pages.

Most experts recommend one page. This translates into a few short paragraphs. Most freelancers agree on keeping it to one page, and it's an excellent guideline for beginners.

But you'll notice in the sample query letters in this eBook that I often use two pages. This hasn't hurt me. Many editors have even accepted three page query letters when I've had to elaborate about the topic.

My advice is to make the query letter as long as it needs to be to describe to the editor what's important for making his decision. That might take three paragraphs or three pages. But don't ramble. Make sure every word you include is important.

No matter what the length of your query letter, there's one thing that's certain: **by the end of your first paragraph, editors will have already decided whether they'll take your article or not.**

A strong opener is more important than the length of your query letter.

## Target your publication.

To get a feel for what kind of stories a travel magazine publishes, read recent back issues and the writer's guidelines. You can usually find the writer's guidelines online.

Nothing annoys editors more than a query that is inappropriate for their magazine. If a magazine does not publish first person travel stories, for example, this is not the place for your personal experience about head hunting with a Borneo jungle tribesman.

Writing first person narratives is a common beginning travel writer's mistake, and I'm sorry to tell you, it doesn't have much appeal.

Even though you had a blast in London, zipping around on the tube, feeding the pigeons on Trafalgar Square and going on that tour of the Tower of London, readers don't want to know about it.

Narratives that read, "First we went to see Big Ben, and then we took the subway to Temple Bar and Somerset House, and then we went to Greenwich", don't really knock the socks off your readers.

Unless your personal experience included meeting Queen Elizabeth II in a haberdasher's shop and being invited to the Palace for a cup of tea and private tour, readers will not be interested. Don't pitch them.

Another common mistake is for beginners to pitch foreign travel stories to magazines that only publish North American stories—and vice versa.

Also, do some research to see if the magazine you're targeting has run an article recently about your proposed destination. If a recent story has been published, yours will likely be rejected. Try pitching different magazines that haven't just run a story on the topic or destination.

## Use the correct submissions procedure.

You'll find submissions information in the writer's guidelines for each magazine. These guidelines are usually posted on the magazine's website. Always read the writer's guidelines before you put your query letter together.

The writer's guidelines will often specify the desired word count, how to submit the query, what they pay writers and other important information. (http://www.pitchtravelwrite.com/writers-guidelines.html.)

## Address the editor by name if possible.

Magazine editors come and go so it's always a good idea to confirm the editor's name before you send your query. You can find names located on the masthead of the latest issue of the magazine or on the magazine's website.

You can also make a phone call to the magazine and ask for the editor's name. Be sure to confirm the correct spelling when doing this over the phone.

If you've exhausted all possibilities and still can't locate the editor's name, address your query letter to "Dear Editor" or "Dear Sir or Madam". If you have a good story idea, it's likely the editor won't be offended that you didn't use his/her name.

## Make your sentences highly descriptive.

You only have a few sentences to paint a picture for the editor, so go overboard with your active verbs and strong descriptions. Paint a picture of the destination to take the editor there, or at least give him a glimpse of the place.

Make sure the editor will want to read the story by dazzling him with clear, descriptive writing. Use the same active verbs and strong descriptions as you plan to use in your story.

Using an example from my Pere LaChaise article:

"Sculptors, art aficionados and tourists wander the quiet, uneven gray-cobble stone labyrinth of streets in this necropolis, admiring the hundreds upon hundreds of superbly wrought, water-streaked bronzes, green weathered copper statues, and flawlessly carved white marble statues of perfect angels, nymphs, and small children".

One thing to avoid in your query letters is clichés. Here are some words and phrases to avoid: paradise, azure blue waters, emerald green fields, steamy jungles, villages nestled high on the mountaintops, an Eden-like setting, a kaleidoscope of colors, teeming with people, spectacular, astonishing, beautiful, bucolic, verdant. You get the idea.

While these phrases and words may be descriptive, and thus very enticing to the novice travel writer, they've been beaten to death. Trust me on this! Avoid them like the plague (clichés intended).

Leave the clichés for the tourist brochures. You're writing a story to give readers a sense of the place, not a guidebook narrative. Give them some deeper, more emotional and vivid descriptions.

## Appeal to the editor's emotions.

If I'm writing about an evocative place, I'll use all sorts of emotive imagery. This can be difficult for some beginning writers, but it will help get your ideas across to editors and sell your story.

Here's an example from a query letter that got my article about the American Military Cemetery at Normandy into the *Sunday Oregonian* newspaper:

"Visitors to this cemetery always remember the deeply moving sight of hundreds of perfectly aligned rows of white crosses stretching away over dozens of acres of deep green grassed fields, and the peaceful serenity of the cemetery locations. They come away knowing this country has never forgotten the ultimate sacrifices these young soldiers made during World War Two".

## Appeal to all the editor's senses.

We have five senses: sight, sound, taste, touch, and smell. Most writers tend to hit sight and sound fairly well in their descriptions.

To paint a more vivid picture, try describing things using all your senses. If you can't use them all, use as many as make sense.

Here's an example from a query letter to a beer aficionado magazine that resulted in a cover story about Belgium's Top Ten Beer Festivals:

"Beer experts swirl, sniff, sip, and taste everything from dark, potent, heady Trappist beers to light subtly flavored summer ales, many taking copious notes after each sampling. This can be serious business".

## Show enthusiasm and passion for your proposed story.

Wherever you can slip it in, show your excitement about the topic you are proposing. Attempting to sell anything without passion is obvious to the editor. And enthusiasm is contagious. So don't be afraid to show your interest and enthusiasm.

Here's a comment I received from one editor: "Your passion is certainly encouraging; we love to work with passionate writers".

## Demonstrate your expertise by using examples & facts.

For a query to be short-listed by an editor, your entire pitch should be thoroughly researched and well written. It must look professional and be professionally presented.

Use facts from your research to show the editor you know your topic. Facts such as how many tourists visit the place each year, how tall the spire on the cathedral is, or how many miles of sandy beach often enhance a story and prove you know something about the place. Present the facts within the context of your query as part of the story.

Writers who can uncover less known, unique details are like gold to editors. Just make sure you double-check your facts before submitting your query. Many magazines have a fact checking process built into their process. If your facts are questionable, you will lose credibility with an editor.

Here's an example from a query letter that got my story about American Military Museums in Normandy into the *Kitsap Sun*:

"Along this mix of flat sandy beaches, sloping white sand dunes, towering precipitous cliffs, and small seaside villages, a cottage industry of more than twenty-five World War Two museums have sprung up. Of these, nine are about American divisions or the American landings, and I've been to them all". You can see from this example that the facts are melded into the content, not presented as dry statistics.

Finally, let me address an issue that is part of travel writing myth. There seems to be a feeling that unscrupulous editors will steal your story idea and write the story themselves or assign another writer to do the piece. I can assure you, this is unlikely.

Editors are too busy to write articles for their own magazine, and will not assign your story to someone else. Why would they? You have shown yourself to be the expert on the topic, so why would they bring in someone else who isn't qualified to write your story? It just doesn't make sense. So when you're writing your query, make sure you have provided all the details you think necessary, and don't hold anything back.

## Avoid wishy-washy phrases.

Using phrases such as "your readers might find this interesting" indicates a certain amount of doubt in your mind, which is transmitted to the editor. "Might" is a weak word.

Avoid weak words like might, could, should, and may in a query letter (and in your articles). Always use strong words like, "this article *will* interest your readers because . . . . ."

Sounding confident and professional is important. You're trying to impress an editor on the basis of a short letter, so use positive, strong words.

Another phrase to avoid is "I've never been published before". If you are a beginner, use experience and/or knowledge for credibility. Never tell the editor you have not been published before.

You will see a couple of sample query letters that follow that show how I used my experience and knowledge for credibility, instead of bylines, to prove why I'm qualified to write the article.

## Be flexible about article length.

Many times an editor will require a shorter or longer article. Say something like, "This article will be 1200-1500 words, but I'm happy to work to your requirements". Always mention you'll be flexible and work to the editor's suggestions. You'll see this statement in my query letter samples.

And always mention when you're able to provide photographs with your article. Editors do not always pay for photos, but having them often clinches the deal. Editors hate having to fish around for photographs, so by providing your own photos with your story you've made their life easier. And sometimes you'll be pleasantly surprised by how much extra you can earn with photos. So always mention them if you have photos available.

## Spell out your credentials but don't ramble on.

One of the biggest misconceptions among novice travel writers is the belief that academic credentials are required to write an article, or that it's necessary to state your credentials at the beginning of the query letter.

The story idea is the most important part of the query letter, so that goes first.

Leave your credentials and qualifications for the end of the query letter. If this makes you feel uncomfortable, I can only say that editors are far more interested in the story than your credentials.

You will lose the editor immediately if you lead with your credentials.

Editors look first for good writing and a great topic. These overshadow your credentials in their eyes. But don't forget to mention how many times and where you've been published at the end of your query letter.

One final, important note: never lie about your credentials.

## Be professional.

Query letters are written with the same rules as any other letter – using formal terms such as Mr. or Ms. Don't use the editor's first name or act in a familiar, informal way as if you and the editor were at a bar together last night  - unless you really were!

Editors are looking for writers who are dependable and deliver their articles on time. They appreciate a well-written query that will help them fill a gap in their magazine with good content and offer their readers interesting, valuable information.

Address your query like any other professional letter.

- ∞ Use black text and normal font
- ∞ Put your name and contact details at the top
- ∞ Don't add a photo of yourself
- ∞ No pictographs of inkwells, suitcases, Eiffel Towers or passports, and
- ∞ Definitely no smileys, pink fonts, or colored backgrounds.

## Spelling counts.

Spell-check your query letter! You're a writer, so spell everything correctly. Same goes for grammar. Your "spelling and grammar check" are a good start to help you identify corrections. But don't stop there. Next read through your query and cut any unnecessary or redundant words to make it "tighter" and more readable.

The same goes for your story after you've received the assignment. Readability is important! (http://www.pitchtravelwrite.com/readability.html)

On several occasions I've been asked to edit my story down by a few hundred words to meet the editor's space requirements. My first thoughts are "Well, the story is going to suffer". However, as I apply the scalpel to my article, I'm always amazed at how I can trim some fat here and there. Inevitably the story reads better for it.

Use your query letters as practice in communicating your ideas with accuracy and clarity.

# AFTER THE QUERY LETTER

## Following Up With the Editor

One of the most asked questions is: How long after you send the pitch should you wait to follow up with the editor? The standard answer to this question is, "Whatever the writer's guidelines tell you". This can vary tremendously. Some editors will tell you to feel free to follow up two weeks after you send your query, and others will tell you to wait two months.

However, from my experience, you can safely assume that if you have not heard back from the editor within a month, 99% of the time he or she is not interested in your article.

On the other hand, if the editor likes your story, you will receive a response within a few weeks, at the very longest. I've sometimes heard back from editors within ten minutes of sending my pitch. And the most common response times to my query letters is between two days and two weeks.

These days, most editors don't bother sending rejection emails. Some editors still do, but many editors consider this an optional task. You may feel like this is unprofessional on the editors part , and I agree. But some editors receive dozens or hundreds of query letters each week and responding to queries that don't interest them has become an unimportant task.

I believe that following up with editors is a massive waste of time. I don't do it, and I recommend that you don't bother to do it, either. There are a number of reasons that I don't follow up:

First of all, I send out so many simultaneous queries that 90% of the time an editor will respond, wanting my story. Once the story is accepted by an editor, I'm done. I've sold the story. Following up with the other editors isn't necessary.

Next, I send out so many queries that it would kill huge amounts of time if I did follow up with all of the editors. After sending out a batch of queries, if I don't hear back from any editors I do one of two things: either fire out the query to a different batch of publications on my list, or I think about what I can change about my query letter to get a positive response.

I've talked with other travel writers about following up, and they tell they may have picked up one or two stories over the years by following up, but not enough to make it a worthwhile permanent procedure.

Considering that the main currency of freelance writers is time, I just don't see enough evidence to make it standard practice in my writing business. I've got better things to do with my time.

I also believe most editors get annoyed with overanxious writers bugging them about a query they submitted several weeks ago.

## Dealing with Rejection

When an editor does take the time to reply to your query letter, often it's a rejection. Is rejection bad? No!

I've read all sorts of platitudes about how to deal with rejection emails from editors. The first thing I must say is, it's not personal, it's business. It just doesn't happen to be a good fit for the magazine right now. So what?

Some people make it sound as if getting a rejection letter from an editor is like being marched in front of a firing squad, or being told that you're the world's number one loser, or that your query ideas are worthless.

That's all hogwash. It's a numbers game, and it's important not to feel the slightest bit of remorse, regret, sorrow, or shame when you receive a rejection email.

Think about it this way – rejection is going to happen. Sometimes you have to get some "no's" before you get a "yes". (People write entire books about this topic!) People in sales know this and it's an important concept to internalize. It's not personal. It's part of the sales process.

When you do receive a rejection letter, read through it to see if there's anything you can learn from it, and move on. I've often received very good advice from the editor in a rejection letter – and then used it to my advantage in my next pitch.

I should mention that there are ways to improve your chances of getting your story idea accepted practically every time. I sell 90% of my stories, which means I get an acceptance letter for almost every query I send out. Your query letter is only part of the sales process. There are techniques beyond the scope of this eBook that will improve your chances of selling your story. My freelance writing manual, "The Complete Guide to Marketing and Selling Your Travel Articles" details the different ways to get such a high acceptance rate. (See "Writer's Resources" chapter for more information on this guide!.)

There's one last piece of advice about sending out query letters. If you're ever in doubt about whether to send a query letter to a particular magazine – and you're not sure it's a good fit – send it! I've been constantly amazed at how many magazines I thought were long shots that snapped up my stories.

Conversely, there have been many magazines that I thought were a perfect fit who have completely ignored my pitches. Certainly choose the magazines that you think are the best fit for your story. But when in doubt, send it anyway.

# QUERY LETTER FORMAT AND SEQUENCE

Here's the query letter sequence that I recommend. Many of the items are self-explanatory, but I'd like to point out the technique that is most successful in getting the editor's attention. I call it the **Direct Pitch Technique ™** because it puts your sales pitch first. I don't believe in wasting the editor's time and so I present my story idea in the first paragraph, and I recommend that you do the same. (http://www.pitchtravelwrite.com/query-letter-strategies.html)

Here are all the details in the order that I recommend:

**Today's date**

**Your contact details**  (name, street address, city, state, zip code, phone number and web address)

**Editor's address**

**Salutation**  (Dear Mr. Hemingway)

**First paragraph - what the story is about.**

This is your introduction and tells about the subject of your proposed article and angle you plan to take. Keep it clear and concise.

**Second paragraph - elaborate on the topic.**

Make this very descriptive. It describes the content and appropriateness of your story idea for the magazine. Some writers use bullet points here to illustrate the content of the proposed story.

**Third paragraph (and more if necessary).**

Focus on the editor's needs and why this story will be a good fit for the magazine, telling why the readers would be interested in this information.

**Why you are uniquely qualified to write this story.**

Describe your credentials, practical experience, education, and past bylines that make you an expert on the subject.

Tell the editor where he can find samples of your stories, or "clips". Ideally this is your writer's website.

Your final statement should also mention the anticipated word length of your article if you haven't already mentioned it. Be sure to say you're flexible to suit the editor's needs. This is also where mention your gallery of photos to accompany the article, if you have them.

**The close.**

What happens next? Will you wait to hear from the editor? Will you call the editor in two weeks time? State clearly the next step. Then close the letter and sign your name.

# GETTING PAID

I have a few words of advice before we get to the sample query letters:

Never mention in your query letter what you expect to be paid for the article. If you've read the writers guidelines, you will often know what the magazine pays their writers. If not, when the editor contacts you, says he likes your story and wants you to go ahead and write it, he will email back with his offer. Then you can enter the elaborate little negotiation dance that ensues between writer and editor.

This is when you clarify the length of the story (how many words), how much he can pay and when (payment and terms), and when he needs it (the deadline). These are the big three things to clarify and agree on before you forge ahead and write the article. Always make sure you agree on these three things before you write the story.

Here's what happens when these things aren't discussed. You might receive a check much smaller than you were hoping for. Or, even worse, you might not get paid at all. Yes, this does happen.

The good news is that it only needs to happen once before you remember to negotiate the big three items before writing and submitting the story. Some writers draft a contract for the editor to sign, others use email correspondence as their letter of agreement. Some editors send a contract to the writer. As a freelancer you'll need to decide your own policies and procedures.

# TWENTY SAMPLE QUERY LETTERS

Here are twenty query letters that worked for me. They all resulted in the story being published, many in prestigious print magazines and one online example.

Some pitches are to regional magazines, while others are to national or international publications. And in most cases these stories paid very well, a few of them four figure payouts.

When you purchased this e-book, it was because you wanted to know how I managed to sell over 1000 articles to 200 different magazines, newspapers, in-flights, on-boards, and online travel magazines. So, all the sample query letters were crafted by me.

I've purchased a variety of books with sample query letters and was surprised when their samples were purchased from, or donated by, other freelance writers. I was disappointed and somewhat suspicious about this as I was interested in what made the author successful, not a random batch of writers. So all the query letters you'll find here are mine, and resulted in a sale.

As you read through these query letters you'll come to realize that writing a good query letter is not rocket science. I believe you should rely more on common sense than sheer writing talent to sell your story idea.

A query letter is a sales pitch, not a literary work.

My query letters are simple and easy to read. Editors don't want to struggle to figure out what you're pitching. A well-written query letter is not complicated. It presents a clear picture to the editor and is not confusing.

Most of the query letters here are not elaborate. Nor are they written in epic Shakespearian prose, although I did get carried away in a few of them!

Remember, the query letter is a sample of your writing, and the editor will assume this is how you normally write.

As you read through these query letters, you might think, "I could have written that", and that's what I'm hoping will happen. My query letters follow a simple formula that you'll recognize as you read through them.

Use these query letters as a guideline and for ideas when drafting your own pitches. Use the format, make adjustments to suit your own style, and insert the facts and figures about your story and your background to make it your own.

Some of these query letters are simple emails that I used to pitch story ideas to editors. In other words, they were "quickie" pitches that I inserted into emails when I was corresponding with an editor over something else. I've noted the situations that deviate when I introduce the letters.

Despite this casual approach, they resulted in published articles, proving how much easier it is to get an editor to accept your pitches once they've had the pleasure of working with you previously. (It's up to you to make sure it is a pleasure!)

I've introduced each query letter with a story, so that you can get some idea of the context of the letter. You'll also see some comments about the stage of my writing career when I wrote the letter.

When I think it will be helpful, I explain the nuts and bolts of the query letter so you can understand more easily how and why I wrote it.

You will also notice that there are many similarities among these query letters.

I believe in working from a template for all my repetitive tasks. A query letter is a repetitive task, so I use a basic template and then make adjustments to suit the publication, the topic and the circumstances.

Having a template for all of your repetitive work will save you time and allow you to earn more in the long run. I've written about this on my website PitchTravelWrite.com where you can learn several way s to be more productive and create more time in your day.
(http://www.pitchtravelwrite.com/increase-productivity-create-more-time.html)

Finally, I've included the magazine where these articles were published but I've left the editors names off the letters. Editors change so frequently that I don't want to mislead anyone who might be using this book.

To find the editor's name for any of these publications, access their website or look in the masthead of their magazine. That way you'll be working with current information.

# A FASCINATING DAY TRIP: REGIONAL MAGAZINE

This query letter marked my breakthrough into the top Pacific Northwest regional travel magazine, Northwest Travel. It's a lengthy query letter because I really wanted to give the editor a sense of the place. And it paid off.

The pitch section of this query letter is nine paragraphs long. Highly unusual and definitely different from the norm, yet it worked.

Since this article was published, I've had dozens of articles in this magazine. I'm regularly invited on press trips around the Pacific Northwest as a result of my visibility in this magazine, and a few other regionals.

To: Mr. <Editor's Name>, Editor, Northwest Travel Magazine

Subject: Query re article "Roslyn's Rich Vein of History"


Dear Mr. <Editor's Name>,

I'd like to submit a piece telling Northwest Travel readers about a fascinating living ghost towns and its atmospheric cemetery, just off Interstate-90 in Washington.

For bored and jaded Seattleites wanting to get away from it all, yet who want to stay close to home, Roslyn, Washington, is a perfect antidote.

If you want to wallow in the sentimental, fascinating and at times tragic history of this still largely intact old coal wooden mining town, dating back to 1886, you'll strike gold here.

The article will be 1200 words, describing the rich history and interesting sights in this largely preserved and restored wooden clapboard town of 1,000 people, still looking much as it was in the late 1800's.

I'll show your readers the historic buildings in the center of town that was itself designated a National Historic District in 1978. And the amazing historical cemeteries where you'll find segregated plots dedicated to people from most of the 28 nations that were lured here from the old world by Northern Pacific Railway's subsidiary coal company. These graveyard sites are collectively acknowledged as the best historic cemetery in the entire state of Washington.

The twenty five separate cemeteries, dating from 1887, are a poignant legacy from the old world, where Croatians, Poles, Italians, Slovakians, and many other nationalities and fraternal lodges like the orders of the Moose, Eagles, Odd fellows, Knights of Pythias, and others, were buried. Reminders all, of why the downtrodden and oppressed came from Europe to the new world—to get away from the ethnic fighting that prevailed back home.

To add to the mystery of this atmospheric town, set in a rocky gully surrounded by a forest of green mountain firs, is the tragic coal-mining explosion in which 49 miners perished nearby—there's a monument to them right in the center of town. Right across the street is the 1899 Brick Tavern, supposedly Washington's oldest operating saloon, with its still operating shiny brass spittoon gutter winding past the front of the bar.

And to add to the magic mix that is Roslyn, I'll tell how this town became famous from

1990-95 as the filming site for Cicely, Alaska, in the quirky television series Northern Exposure. And how Roslyn became a ghost town when, in the 1930's Roslyn shrank from 4,000 people to almost nothing when coal fell victim to the widespread use of electricity and fuel oil.

A walking tour through Roslyn along Pennsylvania Avenue up to the cemeteries, and back through its side streets with their restored old original white painted buildings brings home to the visitor what a special place it is. There's enough here to keep the interest of adults and kids alike, with restaurants serving better food than you'd have the right to expect from such a small town. Roslyn makes a memorable outing.

Your readers will enjoy learning about a truly different town they can visit for a day, or a fun break from driving along I-90, or to stay overnight in one of the town's several B & B's. I have many quality photographs of the various sights in Roslyn to accompany the article.

I'm a full time professional freelance travel and writer with more than 400 articles appearing in over 130 regional, national and international magazines, newspapers, e-zines and In-Flights. Travel magazines publishing my work include Go World Travel, Scotland Magazine, Britain Magazine, Country Magazine, Northwest Travel, South Sound, Columbia Gorge, Gorge Guide, Zymurgy, Tourist Travel, Travellady, Travel Post Monthly, Classic Boat, Blue Water Sailing, 48 North, Mysteries, Renaissance Magazine, and New Zealand Sunday News. Clips are available upon request.

Please see my website for samples of my travel writing at www.Roy-Stevenson.com.

Thank you for consideration of this article. Please contact me if this piece looks like a good fit your magazine. I look forward to hearing from you.

Best Regards,

Roy Stevenson

# AN UNUSUAL STORY ANGLE: NICHE MAGAZINE

This query letter got my "Paris Catacombs" story placed in a print magazine and eventually in an online travel magazine. The example here is to show that pitching for an online magazine or website isn't any different than pitching for a print publication.

Understandably, everyone who's been to Paris wants to write about everything they saw. It's a magnificent city with dozens of marvelous attractions.

But, Paris roundup stories have been beaten to death for decades, and editors want to publish something different than the usual stuff.

I thought about what I saw that was different, off the beaten path, and came up with the idea of pitching the underground Paris Catacombs.

The first four paragraphs paint an atmospheric portrait of these bizarre and macabre catacombs, and cemented the story's chances of being accepted for publication.

To: <Editor's Name>, Editor, Renaissance Magazine

Subject: Query re article "The Subterranean Empire of Paris's Ancient Catacombs:

Dear Mr. <Editor's Name>,

I'd like to submit a piece telling Renaissance readers about "The Subterranean Empire of Paris's Ancient Catacombs".

Underneath Paris, the City of Lights, there is a darker world. Every year over 150,000 curious people visit part of a labyrinth of 186 miles of eerie ancient subterranean tunnels known as the catacombs, twenty meters below the bustling streets of Paris. These catacombs are one of the most extraordinary places in the world, and not well known to most tourists.

Walking through this huge underground crypt is like entering another realm where the surreal is normal, amidst enormous piles of macabre grinning skulls and aged yellowed bones. This astonishing necropolis contains the bones of 6 million bodies.

How they got there is another fantastic story. They were disinterred from 30 cemeteries around Paris centuries ago.

But these catacombs are not just for the macabre minded.

The sense of Paris's layers of history is so strong it's tangible as you wander through this enormous mausoleum. The visitor wonders who these people were, what they did, how old they were, and how they died. It's a very personal experience.

This 1300 word article tells what it is like to walk through the narrow dimly lit tunnels past row upon row of neatly stacked bones and skulls, and about the fascinating history of the catacombs that reflects the history of Paris herself. I'll also mention the secretive urban explorers who roam the catacombs at night.

Your readers will enjoy reading about a place in Paris that most tourists don't know about. For people who've seen all the standard attractions in Paris and are looking for something unusual, the catacombs are perfect. The article is ready now, and I have photographs to accompany it.

I'm a full time professional freelance travel writer with more than 400 articles appearing in over 130 regional, national and international magazines, newspapers, e-zines and In-Flights.

Military and travel magazines publishing my work include Artilleryman, Classic Military Vehicles, Military Machines International, Military Magazine, Go World Travel, Scotland Magazine, Britain Magazine. Clips are available upon request.

Please see my website for samples of my travel writing at www.Roy-Stevenson.com.

Thank you for consideration of this article. Please contact me if this piece looks like a good fit your magazine.

I look forward to hearing from you at your convenience.

Best Regards,

Roy Stevenson

# SELL YOUR STORY INTERNATIONALLY: SPECIALTY MAGAZINE

This is a highly respected U.K. print magazine read widely throughout the U.K. and North America.

I was thrilled to see my story in this magazine. It's a good example of how to sell a travel story to a specialty magazine - in this case a sailing magazine. It's also an international magazine.

I'd been on a yachting/sailing writing binge when I sent this query, as I was enjoying the sailing life and going on various wine and beer cruises on a schooner.

This nicely constructed query letter has four solid pitch paragraphs describing the Schooner Rendezvous. It ends with the standard listing of my bylines and an invitation to view my writer's website, that has plenty more writing samples.

To: Mr. <Editor's Name>, Editor, Classic Boat Magazine

Subject: Query re article "The Pacific Coast Windjammer Fleet Schooner Rendezvous, Tacoma, Washington".

Dear Mr. <Editor's Name>,

I'd like to submit a piece telling your readers about the Pacific Coast Schooner Rendezvous in Tacoma, Washington.

On April 24 & 25, Tacoma's renown Thea Foss Waterway will be packed, bow to stern, with over 15 magnificent antique schooners from along the Pacific coast. With their fore-and-aft sails billowing from two tall wooden masts, these beautifully crafted ships, mostly built between 1900 and 1920, will bring a bygone era of sailing back to nautical fans.

I'll tell the story behind this inaugural schooner rendezvous, organized by the newly formed Puget Sound Schooner Association (PSSA), and where these superb ships come from. I'll describe their maritime history when schooners were the most important North American ships, used mainly for coastal trade and fishing.

I'll also show the interesting personal histories of some of the schooners. The Ragland, for example, was owned by singer Neil Young. The Zodiac was owned by the heirs of the Johnson & Johnson Company. Other notable schooners that will be at Tacoma include Kia Ora, Martha, Spike Africa, Grail, Suva and Lucky Star.

These wooden hulled ships are worth millions of dollars, and outfitted with breathtaking fixtures and furniture. Not many people get a chance to explore schooners, so I'll take your readers inside them, and describe their interiors. I have access to all of the schooners and their captains, arranged by the PSSA.

This article will be of great interest to your readers because schooners are an occasionally glimpsed relic of the past, usually on the distant horizon, and most sailors would dearly love to learn more about them.

I can have this story to you in the first week of May. This piece will be 1500-1800 words and I'll be happy to write it to your specifications. I'll have several dozen high-resolution color photographs to accompany this article, some of which I am hoping will be of cover quality.

I'm a professional, full-time freelance travel writer with more than 400 articles appearing in over 120 regional, national and international magazines, newspapers, e-zines and in-flights. I write the monthly marina/destinations piece for 48 Degrees North yachting magazine in Seattle.

My work has been published in Columbia Gorge, Gorge Guide, Kitsap Sun, Mid-Columbian, South Sound, Sunday Oregonian, Northwest Travel, Sculpture, Tourist Travel, Travel Post Monthly, Go World Travel, Scotland, Beers-of-the-World and Open Skies.

For clips of my work please go to www.Roy-Stevenson.com.

Thank you for consideration of this article. Please contact me if this piece looks like a good fit your magazine.

I look forward to hearing from you at your convenience.

Best Regards,

Roy Stevenson

# USE ACTIVE VERBS: INFLIGHT MAGAZINE

This query marked my breakthrough into Inflight magazines, that holy of holies for freelance travel writers. I received a nice payout for this piece and wrote an article that remains one of my favorites to this day.

In your query letter you only have a few sentences to paint a picture for the editor. Use enough descriptive language to take the editor there and give him a glimpse of the place. Use the same active verbs and strong adjectives as you plan to use in your story.

When you look at the letter you'll see how I got carried away with my descriptive language. It went on and on. The pitch took up six lengthy paragraphs!

This query letter weighs in at two pages, considered very lengthy in contemporary freelance travel writing—yet another example where breaking the "rules" paid off for me. It may seem over the top, but it worked, so I'm including it here.

After all, selling the article is how we measure our success.

To: Mr. <Editor's Name>, Editor, Emirates Open Skies Inflight Magazine

Subject: Article about "The Superb Sculptures at Paris's Pere Lachaise Cemetery".

Dear Mr. <Editor's Name>,

I'd like to submit a piece telling Open Skies Magazine readers about "The Superb Sculptures at Paris's Pere Lachaise Cemetery".

Every year almost two million people stroll for hours among exquisitely carved life sized metal and marble statues in a 109-acre green memorial park in Paris's well-heeled Republique district. They come to see what are considered by many to be the finest collection of funeral sculptures in the world.

Sculptors, art aficionados and tourists wander the quiet, uneven gray cobble stoned labyrinth of streets, admiring the hundreds upon hundreds of superbly wrought water-streaked bronze and green weathered copper statues, and smooth flawlessly carved white marble statues of perfect angels, nymphs, and small children.

The superb quality of the artistic figurines and life sized metal and marble busts of the deceased would make any contemporary sculptor proud--indeed many of the statues are the result of some of Paris's foremost 19th century sculptors.

The article will be 1500-2000 words, describing the incredible range of sculptures at Pere Lachaise, the emotions they reveal, and the famous people who are buried here including many renowned artists and sculptors. I'll also briefly explain the fascinating and dramatic history of this artistic necropolis.

The sculptures express an extremely powerful and wide range of human emotion. The busts, marble carvings and statues portray everything from joy at being in their final resting place in heaven, to grief at the deceased's departure, including one particularly heart-rending life-sized bronze piece of a young boy, obviously taken before his time. He sits on a throne-like chair, garbed in 19th century clothing, his faithful dog standing on its rear legs nuzzling fondly at its master's chest.

Sublime marble busts gaze at you with enigmatic smiles. Macabre green copper, cloaked figures beckon you into the underworld. And who can forget the anguish of the holocaust memorial sculptures tucked away in one corner of the cemetery? The Natzweiler-Strufhof memorial shows a life-size skeletal bronze corpse, ribs protruding, lying on its back, right arm across its chest-it lies atop a platform of coarse, roughly hewn granite stones. I t's as if the artists who created these abstract and realistic monuments were in the camps themselves, so emotive are their works, and so perfectly have they captured the appalling torment and suffering of the prisoners. These are some of the world's finest examples of agony ever portrayed in sculpture.

Surprisingly, Pere Lachaise also boasts an array of sensuous and erotic sculptures that bring together the powerful emotions of death and sensuality. There's a special reason why this particular cemetery was allowed virtually unlimited creative expression—I'll explain that in the article.

I have a number of high quality photographs of some of the beautiful sculptures at Pere Lachaise. I've just returned to the U.S. after living two years in Brussels, Belgium, only 1.5 hours from Paris by fast train, where I spent many weeks. I've even led tours around the city of lights.

This article will be of great interest to readers of Open Skies Magazine because Paris is a major destination for your fliers. It will show them one of the most fascinating art cemeteries in the world and tell them more about the particular pieces found there—they'll want to visit Pere Lachaise Cemetery.

I'm a full time professional freelance travel writer with more than 400 articles appearing in over 130 regional, national and international magazines, newspapers, e-zines and In-Flights. Military and travel magazines publishing my work include Artilleryman, Classic Military Vehicles, Military Machines International, Military Magazine, Go World Travel, Scotland Magazine, Britain Magazine, Country Magazine, Northwest Travel, South Sound, Columbia Gorge, Gorge Guide, Zymurgy, Tourist Travel, Travellady, Travel Post Monthly, Classic Boat, Blue Water Sailing, 48 North, Mysteries, Renaissance Magazine, New Zealand Sunday News. Clips are available upon request.

Please see my website for more samples of my travel writing at www.Roy-Stevenson.com.

Thank you for consideration of this article. Please contact me if this piece looks like a good fit your magazine. I look forward to hearing from you at your convenience.

Best Regards

Roy Stevenson

# BREAKING INTO A NEW GENRE: ART MAGAZINE

Many experts say you should specialize in one field for your freelance writing. I disagree.

I believe it's possible to specialize in several areas of interest and be well published in them all, if you're prepared to work hard. I've been recognized for my writing in running and triathlon training, fitness & health, travel, luxury resorts and spas, military history, classic cars, communications, food, wine & beer, and a few other fields.

Here's an example of an enjoyable assignment I followed up on while speaking at a travel writer's conference in San Francisco. I had my trip lined up and a friend at the Community College where I was teaching strongly recommended that I meet this sculptor, who lives and works just across the bridge in Marin County.

The artist, Al Farrow, was doing some interesting work with quasi-military and political themes and using lots of dissembled military equipment to make his remarkable sculptures.

I pitched a story about the sculptor and his art to several sculpture and art magazines and landed this assignment with prestigious Sculpture Magazine, which paid well.

Now, I've never written about art before, so was not sure how to go about it. But, I came through just fine, learned a lot, and had a marvelous day in Al Farrow's studio, watching him work and seeing his fascinating cathedrals and mosques.

My pitch is six paragraphs long, and indicates that I did a lot of research about Al Farrow before I pitched my story. I'm sure this is what got my story into print. This brings up a point that I like to emphasize to aspiring travel writers: never be afraid to pitch and write a story in an area you are not familiar with.

It's also important that you have an interest in this area to sustain your motivation while you're researching and writing your story.

You get around unfamiliar topics by consulting with experts in the field, or buying a book or two about the subject, and surfing on the Internet, to find information.

I've become an expert on military vehicles, military history, antique weapons, artillery, and World War II simply by doing lots of reading on these topics. And now I also know a little bit about the art world.

To: Mr. <Editor's Name>, Editor, Sculpture Magazine

Subject: Al Farrow, San Francisco's Renaissance Reliquary Sculptor


Dear Mr. <Editor's Name>,

I'd like to submit a piece on "Al Farrow, San Francisco's Renaissance Reliquary Sculptor". Mr. Farrow has recently gained an international reputation with his controversial Reliquary series, featuring human bones in miniature cathedrals made from guns, bullets, and shell casings. His workshop, in tiny San Rafael, just across the Golden Gate Bridge from San Francisco, is like a cross between an arms and munitions depot and mausoleum, with guns, bullets, drawers of bones and military paraphernalia strewn all over.

With names like Trigger Finger of Santa da Guerra, Study for Mosque Reliquary, and Monument to Surrender, his work has appeared so contentious that several newspaper articles have watered down their descriptions so much they lost the essence of what he's trying to say. In a recent visit to his workshop, Mr. Farrow tells me, "I've always done stuff that's hard to live with. My juxtaposition of war and religion and how they have related through history, and the concept of violence and religion go hand in hand".

My article will describe the evolution of Al Farrow's five superb sculpture series: Dancers, Beggars, Icarus, Africa, and Reliquary. I'll show his main works of each series, describe his workshop, his techniques and how he got into sculpting at the age of 29. And I'll tell your readers about his house, essentially an art museum, absolutely crammed from floor to ceiling in every room with pre-Columbian sculptures, ceramics, and art and artifacts from all over the world.

Mr. Farrow's recent sale of his "Cathedral", an enormous Gothic cathedral made from guns and bullets weighing 1 ton, to San Francisco's famed de Young Museum for $150,000, marked his emergence into the upper echelons of sculpture if money is used as a gauge. However, Al grew up in the slums of New York, "accustomed to being poor", and has always remained true to his beliefs.

I'll talk about the personal side of this intelligent and fascinating 65-year old man, and the extensive research he does before starting a series. He met his wife, a ballet dancer and instructor through ballet lessons he took while researching ballet movement for his dancer series.

Your readers will be interested to know that his reliquary series developed over the years as a natural progression from his earlier works in metal, his "Beggar" series being his second. His drawings of the beggar series have been exhibited alongside Rembrandt's beggar series drawings at exhibitions in Europe—quite a compliment for a beginning artist. And Farrow's work has been shown in Italy, Washington, D.C., New Mexico, Illinois, and at the New York and Miami art fairs. He has a gallery in Brussels courting him to distribute his work in Europe.

I have access to a large number of high-resolution photos of Mr. Farrow's sculptures, plus dimensions, transcripts from a recent interview with him, and access to him anytime.

I'm a freelance writer with over 300 articles published at the regional, national and international level in magazines, newspapers, E-zines, and In-Flights, on art, communications, film festival reviews, history, military history, fitness and health. Clips are available upon request.

Please contact me if you'd like this piece on Al Farrow. Thank you for your consideration of this article. I look forward to hearing from you.

Best Regards,

Roy Stevenson

# NEW WRITER, FEW CREDENTIALS: SPECIALTY MAGAZINE

This query letter was my first pitch to the editor of Renaissance magazine, back in 2007 when I first began my freelance writing career. It was for a travel story about torture museums that I had visited around Europe.

I was thrilled that this story was accepted for publication. It led to an ongoing relationship that still endures—my work is still being published in Renaissance magazine to this day.

Here's more proof that you don't need to sell your travel stories solely to travel magazines. Use your imagination to come up with specialty magazines that might be interested in your off-beat articles.

Renaissance Magazine is aimed at readers who participate in living history reenactments at medieval faires, historical events, architecture, and lifestyle, and fans of all things medieval.

While this magazine may not pay its readers great sums of money, writing for Renaissance magazine has provided me with numerous assignments in Europe. My latest assignments, for example, led to three very pleasant days touring the medieval city of York and a nice road trip around Wales.

These assignments have enabled me to prolong my annual jaunt to Europe into several weeks instead of the usual week or two. And, I've had the opportunity to attend numerous medieval faires in England, on a VIP press pass. The British really do medieval faires well, and I've seen some surreal sights. There's something about visiting a medieval faire where the people speak with broad English accents and are actual descendants of the roles they are playing that creates an irresistible atmosphere.

The special thing about this query letter is that it's clean and gets straight to the point. Since I was new to travel writing, it spells out my writing credentials and why I'm qualified to write this story even though I didn't have many relevant bylines yet.

To:   Mr. <Editor's Name>, Editor, Renaissance Magazine

Subject:  Re: Article about "Torture Museums In Western Europe"

Dear Mr. <Editor's name>,

I'd like to submit a piece telling Renaissance Magazine readers about "Torture Museums In Western Europe". Every year hundreds of thousands of morbidly curious tourists venture into gloomy, dimly lit basements and castles to see torture museums in England, the Netherlands, France and Belgium where they learn about implements of torture used in Medieval Europe.

These forms of punishment were inflicted for being in debt, extracting confessions, practicing the wrong faith (heretics and witches), theft, murder, immoral conduct (prostitution), and any other reason that could be used to make life miserable for the downtrodden in Europe.

The article will be 1500-2000 words and describe the Torture Museums and implements in the Clink Prison Museum and Wax Museum in London, England, The Torture Museum in the Medieval Castle of Carcassonne, France, The Torture Museum in Amsterdam, Netherlands, and the torture displays in Gravenstein Castle, Ghent, Belgium. I have photographs to accompany the article.

I've just spent 2 ½ years living in Brussels and London. Having the luxury of not working during this time I traveled constantly to all things historic throughout Western Europe. The torture museums were too intriguing to pass up and gave me an insight into the reality of European life.

This article will be of great interest to readers of Renaissance Magazine because it will tell them about an aspect of life in medieval and renaissance Europe that is hardly ever publicized. They'll learn about such charming devices as the Neck Violin, the Heretic's Fork, the Thumb Screw, the Pear, the Scavenger's Daughter, the Sling, the Claw, and the Judas cradle.

The article will also make good reading for the armchair travelers in your readership as I'll briefly describe two of the castles where Torture Museums can be found.

I'm a freelance writer with articles published on history, travel and culture, military history, film festival reviews, and fitness and sports. Clips are available on request. You can view one of my latest online pieces about the Paris Catacombs at (link given here)

Thank you for your consideration of this article. I look forward to hearing from you at your convenience.

Best Regards,

Roy Stevenson

# PAINT PICTURES: WORDS & PHOTOS: ADVENTURE MAGAZINE

This query letter landed me a 4-figure payout for an article in Off-Road Adventure Magazine. It was a great travel assignment in England, covering the world's largest military vehicle event. Nirvana!

It's a good example of how you can sell your travel stories to magazines in other genres—in this case, a publication about four wheel drive vehicles.

When I wrote this query letter, I'd been writing successfully for four years and had 400 articles published. My growing confidence in my abilities as a freelance writer is reflected in this letter but the first three paragraphs still spell out my pitch in enticing terms. I paint a good picture of the event with a solid description in the second paragraph.

Notice that I indicate I'm willing to be flexible on what the editor wants in this story. I had never written for this magazine before, so I'm feeling my way about editorial preferences. I'm happy to focus on any aspect of the show that he prefers, or do a general round up piece.

Also note that I offer to provide high-resolution photographs to accompany this piece. And indeed, photos comprised most of this article, with 1000 words wrapped around them.

Another thing I mention in this query is an "Editors Comments" section on my own writer's website (www.roy-stevenson.com). This gives a new editor references for my work, so he or she feels comfortable working with me.

I also display samples of my military (and other genre) articles on the same website. I'm sure the numerous sample articles on my website—plus the "Editors Comments" section—have worked in my favor countless times.

If you haven't yet built your a writer's website, I've described how to do it and what's important on my website in an article named:
"Why Freelance Writers Need a Professional Website"
(http://www.PitchTravelWrite.com/professional-website.html)

Make sure you place some of your articles on your writer's website after they are published. And encourage editors to write some nice testimonials for your website. They're deal clinchers!

To: Mr. <Editor's Name>, Editor, Off-Road Adventures Magazine

Subject: Query re: article, "The War & Peace Show: The Largest and Most Spectacular Military Vehicle Event in the World"

Dear Mr. <Editor's Name>,

I'd like to submit a piece showing your readers the most renowned military vehicle event in the world. For five days every July, thousands of military vehicles descend on the Hop Farm, Beltring, Kent, an hour's drive Southeast of London to take part in a massive show that gathers together one of the most eclectic collections of military vehicles in the world.

Tanks, armoured cars, soft-skinned vehicles, trucks, ambulances, motorcycles, and jeeps, will clatter, clank and thunder their way around courses and stage large-scale battles in front of a huge crowd of military vehicle aficionados. This is the famous War & Peace Show—the Holy Grail of military vehicle conventions.

This year from July 20-24, I will be attending the War & Peace show, watching the various special military vehicle shows like the Wheels of Victory parade for owners of WWII British and Commonwealth Wheeled Vehicles, and the Die Deutsche Parade, a re-enactors group of marching German soldiers, equipment and vehicles. I'll be photographing the tanks and half-tracks in the Convoy of Steel, and watching the U.S. Army trucks in the Red Ball express. And the Jeeps and tanks in the 4 x 4 off road course, and the Motorcycle Rideout of WWII Axis motorcycles, combinations and Kettenkrads.

I'd like to cover the 2011 War & Peace Show for your magazine. I'm happy to focus on any aspect of the show that you prefer, or do a general round up piece. This article will be of great interest to your readers because it is the biggest and best military vehicle show in the world.

I anticipate this piece will be 1500+ words but I'll be happy to write it to your specifications. I will have plenty of high-resolution photos to accompany this article.

I'm a full time professional freelance writer and photographer based in Seattle, Washington, with more than 400 articles published in over 150 regional, national, and international magazines, newspapers, websites and In-flights. I specialize in military vehicles and aviation, military history, fortifications, artillery, weapons, signals and communications, airborne history, and military museums.

To see samples of my military articles please go to www.Roy-Stevenson.com. Please also take a moment to look at the Editor's Comments section on my website.

My military articles have been published in the U.S.A, U.K, Scotland and New Zealand and have appeared in Army Motors, Classic Military Vehicle (UK), Military Machines International (UK), Classic Arms & Militaria (UK), The Artilleryman, Military Magazine, Scale Military Modeller (UK), Strategy & Tactics, World War II Quarterly, Warbird Digest, Aviation History, SpaceFlight (UK), Airborne Quarterly, Renaissance, Scotland Magazine, Sunday Oregonian, Monitoring Times, Popular Communications, South Sound, New Zealand Sunday News, and Kitsap Sun.

I also write the monthly military museum column for Military Magazine and am currently working on a Guide Book about World War II museums in Western Europe.

Thank you for consideration of this article. Please contact me if this piece looks like a good fit for your magazine. I look forward to hearing from you at your convenience.

Best Regards.

Roy Stevenson

# DESCRIBE YOUR READERS: INTERNATIONAL TRAVEL MAGAZINE

This query got my work into Scotland Magazine, an internationally distributed, top shelf travel magazine. You can find this magazine on the shelves throughout the U.K. and North America.

Interestingly, I'd previously had an article accepted for Beers-of-The-World Magazine by the same editor, which may have helped my chances (I'm assuming she remembered my name).

Note that this story combines two of my favorite interests: travel and military history. This was also a cover story (with a great color photograph of Edinburgh Castle on the cover), and I was only in my third year of freelance writing.

This was a nicely written query for such an early stage of my writing career. By this time I was being published in several similar magazines and starting to believe that my writing was good enough to make the "big guns".

It's a short and clean query, straight to the point, and paints a good picture of Edinburgh Castle. There are four paragraphs in the pitch section of this letter.

Pointing out that the story would appeal to tourists, military historians and artillery aficionados was a cunning ploy to show that lots of people would read this story if they published it. It worked.

To: Ms. <Editor's name>, Editor, Scotland Magazine

Subject: Query re article "Edinburgh Castles' Remarkable Gun batteries and Military Museums".

Dear Ms. <Editor's Name>,

I'd like to submit a piece telling Scotland Magazine readers about Scotland's ancient and powerful military tradition, that is seen better in Edinburgh Castle than anywhere else in the country. Tourists, military historians and artillery aficionados find nirvana in this blackened and weathered stone fortress with its five gun batteries and three military museums (including the National War Museum of Scotland). History is tangible in this unique castle.

I'll show your readers how this ancient fortress's military history is part of the national culture by describing its history as a garrison, how it's still used today for ceremonial purposes, and remains the headquarters for the Royal Scots Dragoon Guards, The Royal Regiment of Scotland, and the 5$^{th}$ Regiment Royal Military Police.

And I'll tell about the Scottish War Memorial, the military museums, the gun batteries, the behemoth Mons Meg gun, and the 18$^{th}$ and 19$^{th}$ century Prisons of War exhibit, not to mention the superb views of Edinburgh from the castle ramparts.

This article will be of great interest to your readers because most people going to Edinburgh Castle have little idea of its proud military history, and this story will give them a better idea of what to expect when they visit it.

This piece is ready now, and I can send it to you immediately upon request. I have a number of quality photographs to accompany this article.

I'm a full time freelance travel and military writer with more than 400 articles appearing in over 130 regional, national and international magazines, newspapers, Ezines and In-Flights. Military and travel magazines publishing my work include Artilleryman, Classic Military Vehicles, Military Machines International, Military Magazine, Go World Travel, Scotland Magazine, Britain Magazine, Country Magazine, Northwest Travel, South Sound, Columbia Gorge, Gorge Guide, Zymurgy, Tourist Travel, Travellady, Travel Post

Monthly, Classic Boat, Blue Water Sailing, 48 North, Mysteries, Renaissance Magazine, and New Zealand Sunday News. Clips are available upon request. Please see my website for more samples of my travel writing at www.Roy-Stevenson.com.

Thank you for consideration of this article. Please contact me if this piece looks like a good fit your magazine.

I look forward to hearing from you at your convenience.


Best Regards,

Roy Stevenson

# RESEARCH BEFORE YOU QUERY: SPECIALTY MAGAZINE

Although I pitched it as one story, this query resulted in two separate articles in the same issue of American Cowboy Magazine. Although this is technically not a travel story, I learned about Black American Cowboys while in Denver a few years ago, speaking at a travel writer's workshop.

One day, with a few hours to spare, I slipped away from the conference and visited the Black American Cowboys of the West Museum in Denver. I was fascinated with what I saw.

American Cowboy is a prestigious publication with a wide readership, and I was thrilled to see my work in it.

The stories were about two legendary cowboys, Bass Reeves and Bill Pickett, whom I learned about while visiting the museum. You'll notice that I mention where I got the story idea. It shows that I'm interested enough in cowboys to visit a museum on the subject. Mentioning this seems to add to the authenticity of my query.

I think the query contained some juicy and spectacular information that obviously hooked the editor. This shows the value of doing some solid research before you send your query. I'm a big believer in dropping some dramatic facts in query letters, if appropriate.

After reading my query, the editor asked me write two articles. He placed them in different sections of the magazine.

An editor will often ask you to change or tweak your pitch. If this happens, don't question it and don't make a fuss over it. Simply tell the editor that you'd be delighted to do it, and then get on with your writing.

My query letter was casual, as I'd already been corresponding with him. We were on first name terms, as you can see below …

Hi <Editor's name>,

I have a story idea that I am hoping will be a good fit for American Cowboy magazine. Please read on . . .

A virtually unknown fact about the American West is that 20% of the cowboys that roamed the plains, explored the mountains, drove the cattle, and competed in rodeos, were black men. And their contributions to developing the West are legendary to the historian of the early American West. These black cowboys became cowboys, rodeo wranglers, drovers, lawmen, writers, soldiers, scouts, mountain men, and movie stars.

I'd like to tell the stories of these legends—they are nothing short of amazing. And I'll bet the vast majority of your readers have never heard of these men and the dozens of other famous black cowboys.

Bill Pickett, "The Dusky Demon" was an Indian/Black hybrid, Texas-born. He became the most famous black cowboy entertainer in American history. Appearing in silent movies and stage productions throughout England and the United States, doing trick roping, bull riding, and steer wrestling with the Miller Brothers 101 Ranch and Wild West Show from Ponca City, Oklahoma. He appeared in hundreds of small and large rodeo events in the East and West. He invented the sport of steer wrestling (also called bulldogging). Pickett brought the image of the Black Cowboy to the nation's mass media.

Bass Reeves was the first African American commissioned to serve as a deputy marshal west of the Mississippi River. Born a slave in Paris, Texas and owned by George Reeves, Bass Reeves grew up illiterate and remained illiterate for his entire life. After the Emancipation Proclamation in 1863, Reeves, now free, moved to Van Buren, Arkansas.

For the next thirty-two years Bass Reeves brought to justice over 3,000 criminals and killed fourteen outlaws during his years as a marshal, garnering a reputation as one of the most successful lawmen in the Indian Territory. One of those he captured was Bob Dozier, a murderer and cattle and horse thief who eluded Reeves for several years before being tracked down and killed after refusing to surrender. He also tracked outlaw Tom Story for five years between 1884 and 1889, finally killing him in a gunfight. Reeves was noted for his evenhandedness, honesty and integrity. He tracked down and arrested his own son after a two-week manhunt.

I got this story idea while in Denver last year, speaking at a travel writer's conference. I visited the Black American Cowboys of the West Museum, and was fascinated to learn of the enormous contribution that black cowboys made to the American West. I'd like to use a description of the museum as a portal to writing about these famous black cowboys, their exploits, and the mark they left on the west.

I can offer several high res photos of the museum and its exhibits. I will be using several sources for this story including the following books: The Legend of Bass Reeves, The Negro Cowboys, and Black Frontiers—A History of African American Heroes in the Old West.

This article will be of great interest to your readers because I do not believe anyone has written specifically about black American cowboys before in ACM.

I anticipate this piece will be 1200-1500 words but I'll be happy to write it to your specifications. Where appropriate I will use sidebars to illustrate my story.


Best Regards,

Roy Stevenson

# BREAK THE RULES: INTERNATIONAL TRAVEL MAGAZINE

This query letter led to two full-length feature articles in Australia & New Zealand Magazine, a prestigious and high quality U.K. travel magazine. As this book is aimed at travel writers, this is a great query letter for you to study.

This query letter broke a couple of "rules", proof that you don't always have to do what the "experts" recommend, or what the books tell you to do.

What rules have I broken here?

Most experts will tell you that you're only supposed to query one story idea at a time. I disagree. I make it common practice to query two (and occasionally three) story ideas in my query letters. In fact, multiple submissions form one of the foundations of my travel writing marketing plan. This query pitches story ideas about two different New Zealand cities.

The other rule broken is the length of this query. I wanted to be clear about the variety of activities in each of these tourist towns and I believe this level of detail helped me to land two stories from this one query, along with an invitation to write more stories in the future.

The actual pitch was fifteen paragraphs, considered very lengthy for a query letter. But it worked, proving that not all queries must be short.

These pitches are basically for roundup stories about Rotorua and Queenstown, two of New Zealand's most renowned tourist towns. Roundup stories don't always have an angle, but in this case I suggested one. The angle suggested is to interview some of the New Zealanders who work at these places. I would have done this anyway for some "local color" and quotes, but it's helpful to point it out to the editor.

I did have to do my homework about the various attractions we were planning on visiting, as you can see from the query letter. I probably got lucky with this pitch—the editor had not run anything about these towns for a while, and was looking for roundup stories about them.

To: <Editor's Name>, Editor, Australia & New Zealand Magazine

Subject: Query re article, "New Zealand's Top Two Tourist Destinations: Queenstown and Rotorua".

Dear Mr. <Editor's Name>,

I'd like to submit a piece telling your readers about New Zealand's perennial tourist favorites, Queenstown and Rotorua—but with a twist. Visiting these action-packed towns are almost a requisite for understanding the quintessential New Zealand (and a lot of fun besides), but I'd like to give your readers a sense of the truly unique New Zealand character and culture behind the tourist attractions, by looking at the Maoris and Pakehas (white new Zealanders) who live and work there.

I intend to use the attractions as a metaphor for the "true blue" Kiwi who fronts up to curious tourists every day: the tour guide, the Maori War dancer, the masseuse at a hot pool spa, the sheep shearer at the Agrodome, the sheep farmer in the High Country Sheep Station, the gold panning instructor, the jet boat driver, the boat captain at Milford Sound—you get the idea. The focus of my story will be just as much on the person behind the tour as on the attractions themselves.

This article will be of great interest to your readers because it will go beyond the standard tourist descriptions of the, "We went here and saw this, and then we went there and saw that" variety, to look at the typical New Zealander proudly showing his country off to his tour group or clients.

Having lived in New Zealand for the first 27 years of my life, I am uniquely qualified to write about the culture of the typical New Zealander, whom I can assure you definitely have their quirks.

I will be visiting these famous towns next month (December 2011) and have planned a variety of activities to give me a wide breadth of tourist offerings including some of their latest attractions. Here is a brief of the places I will be visiting.

***Queenstown activities*** *include a cruise on Milford Sound along deep fjords carved from Granite Mountains by a glacier one million years ago, with precipitous sides soaring 5060 feet above. Located in the Fiordland National Park and Te Wai Pounamu World Heritage Site.*

*A Dart River jet safari—an exhilarating jet boat ride down the pristine Dart River wilderness area to the frontier township of Glenorchy*

*A gold mining historical tour that is a cross between a Lord of the Rings backdrop scene tour and a gold mining tour. Includes a walk through Arrowtown, a gold town dating from 1862, visiting the Chinese settlement, seeing the scene where Blackriders gallop through the River in LOTR, walking through native bush to the original site of the gold discovery by William Fox, and gold panning for elf gold.*

*A visit to the renown Mount Earnslaw High Country Station, in the heart of New Zealand high country, on a 4-wheel-drive jeep, to view 5,500 Perendale sheep, 550 Angus breeding cows, 3 working dogs, and interview the station owners and hands.*

***Rotorua activities*** *include visiting the Polynesian Spa: four rock pools of varying temps, overlooking the shore of Sulphur Bay, Lake Rotorua. Spa therapies offered including mud wraps and packs, manuka honey wraps. The Spa's thirteen private pools include cascading pools.*

*The Agrodome: no trip to NZ is complete without getting an idea of the country's agricultural economic engines, sheep and cattle. The Agrodome gives visitors a crash course in sheep shearing, sheep dog demonstrations, and dog trials.*

*Tamaki Maori Village: Hidden in the Rotorua forest, this Maori Village features the Maori haka challenge greeting to newcomers, the Powhiri welcome dance, Maori songs, Maori warriors training for war with traditional weapons and spears. Visit the Maori village houses and watch Maori tattooing (called Moko), and eat a hangi meal, a succulent underground steam-cooked meal of lamb, kumara, potatoes, carrots, chicken, cooked over red hot lava rocks with water poured on them to create steam.*

*Whakarewarewa Village: Set amid a landscape of erupting geothermal activity, hot thermal springs and hot bubbling mud pools is the living Maori village of Whakarewarewa. Features the Pohutu and Prince of Wales Feathers geysers.*

*Rainbow Springs: This wildlife park features NZ's unique wild animals and birds including the reclusive Kiwi. See a bird show, tuatara lizards, native parrots.*

*Hells Gate is Rotorua's fiercest geothermal area and largest active boiling whirlpool, hot mineral pools, geyser, sulphur lake, mud pools, steam baths, steaming fumaroles and mud bath complex at Wai Ora Spa.*

I anticipate this piece will be 1800-2000 words but I'll be happy to write it to your specifications. If you prefer, I will have no problem writing a separate piece about each of these two places to go into more depth about the people and places. I will have plenty of high-resolution photos to accompany this article. Where appropriate I will use sidebars to illustrate my story.

I'm a full time professional freelance travel writer and photographer with more than 600 articles published in over 160 regional, national, and international magazines, newspapers, online magazines and In-flights.

My work has been published the U.S.A., Canada, England, Scotland, Ireland, Australia, and New Zealand and has appeared in *Scotland Magazine, Britain Magazine, This England, Renaissance, Sunday Oregonian, New Zealand Sunday News, Emirates Open Skies In-flight, Beers-of-the-World, Blue Water Sailing, Classic Boat, Coast Food & Arts, Sculpture, Lost Treasure, Northwest Meetings & Events, Popular Communications, Mid-Columbian, Northwest Travel, South Sound, Columbia Gorge, Off-road Adventures, Zymurgy, Mysteries, Kitsap Sun, GoNomad.com, Go World Travel, Tourist Travel, Travellady, Travel Post Monthly, Travelmag.com*, and many other publications.

For clips of my work please go to my writer's website at www.Roy-Stevenson.com. Please also take a moment to look at the Editor's Comments section on my website. Clips are also available upon request.

Thank you for consideration of this article. Please contact me if this piece looks like a good fit for your magazine. I look forward to hearing from you at your convenience.

Best Regards,

Roy Stevenson

# BUILD REPEAT BUSINESS: TOP SHELF HISTORY MAGAZINE

I've had considerable success in finding military and aviation magazines that will publish my travel stories. These magazines have been from Australia, the U.K, and the U.S. Military oriented magazines seem very receptive to well-written stories that have a travel component. And I've landed numerous exciting press trips from these assignments.

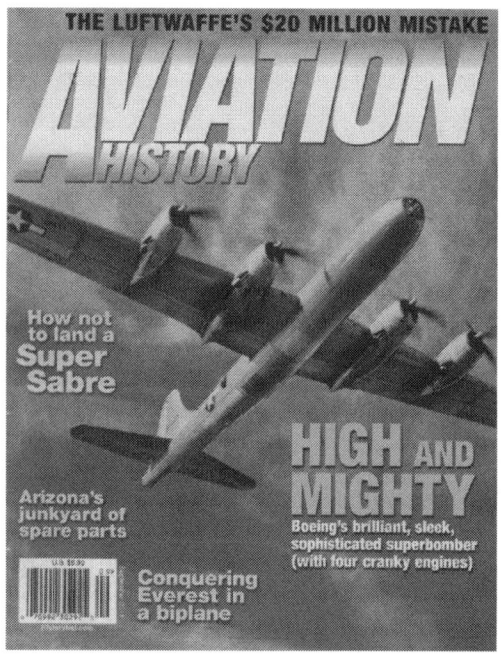

This query letter landed me a feature-length story in Aviation History Magazine, a top shelf U.S. publication. I'd already had a short column piece published in this magazine, so dispensed with the usual pleasantries in my email, and got straight down to business. I reminded the editor of my previous article (very important, because he might not remember me).

My query was for a story about the famous "Boneyard" near Tucson, where the U.S. military stores its outdated aircraft. It's a spectacular sight and I really wanted to write about this place. We ended up getting a personal guided tour around the entire 2,600-acre storage area with the base media officer. She stopped anywhere we wanted, to get up close and personal with the retired aircraft. Great stuff!

My pitch is six paragraphs long, and goes into detail about what's stored at the "Boneyard". My first and second pitch paragraphs paint a picture of the "Boneyard", so I got to utilize my travel writing skills here.

The editor has since taken another of my stories, which shows the power of getting that first story into the barn. Once your first story is published in a magazine, you'll find it's so much easier to get subsequent work into that publication.

To: Mr. <Editor's Name>, Editor, Aviation History Magazine

Subject: Query re article, "Tucson's Famous Aircraft Boneyard—Where the U.S.'s Military Aircraft Go to Die".

Hi <Editor's Name>,

Roy Stevenson here--you ran my piece about the Curtiss Jenny restoration a few months ago.

I'd like to sound you out on another story idea, if I may?

In a vast, flat 2,600-acre section of desert just south of Tucson, Arizona, near Davis-Monthan Air Force Base lie hundreds of neatly arranged rows of 4,400 retired military aircraft—the equivalent of the second largest air force in the world.

These silent titans of the air, with tumbleweed blowing around their landing gear and rattlesnakes slithering underneath, are headed for the aircraft afterlife. They're waiting to be chopped up, sold to other countries, used for target practice or flight instruction, scrapped, melting down, or donated to museums.

I'd like to submit a piece telling your readers about Tucson's famous Aerospace Maintenance and Regeneration Group (AMARG) aircraft Boneyard—where the U.S.'s surplus military aircraft rest while their fate is being decided. It's like walking through a pantheon of U.S. military aviation history as you walk past 700 F-4 Phantoms, behemoth B-52 bombers, F-106, F-111, F-14, F-16, fighter jets, E-2 Hawkeye early warning aircraft, EF-111 Ravens, T-38 Talon chase planes, A-6 Intruders, A-10 Tankbusters, and some unique and rare aircraft like the German Air Force Tornados, and D-21 Drones for the SR-71 Blackbird.

The boneyard is such an impressive sight that it has been used as a backdrop for movies (Transformers: Revenge of the Fallen, Harley Davidson and the Marlboro Man) and music videos like Tom Petty and the Heartbreaker's *Learning to Fly*.

I'll describe the history of AMARG, why this area was chosen as the AMARG storage center, how the aircraft are prepped for storage, what aircraft stand silently in the desert, their eventual fate (including the massive 13,000 lb. guillotine that chops up the B-52s), and some interesting stories told to me by one of AMARG's workers.

I'll also describe the adjacent Pima Air & Space Museum, the largest private air museum in the U.S.A. and the third largest overall, with over 250 aircraft sprawled over 250 acres.

I'll be visiting the AMARG center in late December for a private tour of the Boneyard. This article will be of great interest to your readers because it will show them the amazing sight of all of these "ghost" aircraft and tell about the center and its functions.

I anticipate this piece to be 1500-1800 words and I'll be happy to write it to your specifications. I will have several dozen high res images to accompany this piece.

I'm a full time professional freelance travel writer specializing in military history, aircraft, museums, and vehicles. I have more than 300 articles published 500 times in over 140 regional, national and international magazines, newspapers, e-zines and In-flights. My work has been published in Aviation History, Warbird Digest, Spaceflight, Airborne Quarterly, Classic Military Vehicle, Military Machines International, Classic Arms & Militaria, Military Magazine, Strategy & Tactics, World at War, World War II Quarterly, Scale Military Modeler, and The Artilleryman.

For clips of my work please go to my writer's website at www.Roy-Stevenson.com. Clips are also available upon request.

Thank you for consideration of this article. Please contact me if this piece looks like a good fit for your magazine. I look forward to hearing from you at your convenience.

Best Regards,

Roy Stevenson

# MAKE THE EDITOR SALIVATE: BEER MAGAZINE

A few years ago I was going through my "beer writing" phase, much as Picasso went through his cubism and surrealism phases.

Since this article was published, I've had great success getting my beer travel articles published in several other beer magazines (Beers-of-the-World, Beer Magazine, Beer and Brewer, Zymurgy, Beer connoisseur).

This is proof positive that you don't need to sell your travel articles solely to travel magazines. If you have an angle, like this story, why not try to sell the story to a specialty magazine?

This query letter is about a four-day cruise around the Salish Sea in the Puget Sound, visiting and tasting at some of the region's top microbreweries. Because of my assignment, I got VIP treatment on the cruise and had a great time with the other beer aficionados.

The cruise was even more enjoyable because it was on a beautiful, historic 90-year old schooner, and our chef's gourmet seafood cooking was superb. A memorable trip!

I don't hold back in this query letter. The actual pitch section is seven paragraphs long, and loaded with descriptive language. I wanted to spell out everything that we'd be doing on the beer cruise for the editor.

Remember, I'm trying to sell this story to a "food/wine/beer" publication, so I try to make the editor salivate while he's reading my query. Hopefully it will sound so real that he'll want to publish the story.

When pitching stories to food/wine/beer magazines, don't hold back on your descriptions. You want the editor to see, taste, and smell what you're selling. By doing this, foodie editors can see that you know how to bring the tastes and smells alive.

To:  Mr. <Editor's Name>, Editor, Beer Magazine

Subject:  Query re article, "Oktoberfest Brewery Cruise on Board the Historic Schooner Zodiac"

Dear Mr. <Editor's Name>,

I'd like to submit a piece telling your readers about the Oktoberfest Brewery Cruise aboard the historic schooner Zodiac, in Washington State's beautiful San Juan islands.

Most salty old dogs agree that the Zodiac is the most beautiful boat on the West Coast. Every summer, the magnificent 127-foot long schooner Zodiac hosts two superb brewery tours around the Puget Sound's San Juan Islands. And I'll be on their 4-day brewery and beer tasting cruise from September 30-October 3.

I'd like to show your readers these four glorious days aboard this beautiful 1924 schooner, as we set the sails on the twelve story high topmasts, and cruise from island to island over the deep blue waters of the Salish Sea, visiting the finest breweries in the San Juans.

By day we'll stroll through quaint and picturesque Puget Sound harbor towns like Bellingham, Port Townsend, and Friday Harbor, and visit breweries for tours and tastings; notably the Chuckanut Brewery and Rockfish Pub, Bellingham; and the Port Townsend Brewery.

Every evening, while anchored in peaceful, secluded bays, we'll have beer-tasting sessions where we learn about the varieties and characteristics of Northwest beers, hosted by experts from Seattle's renown Pike Place Brewery, who will have generous samples of their ales to illustrate their presentations.  We'll also brew our own special Schooner Rat IPA on deck, and I'll be happy to provide the recipe for your readers.

Then, to cap off the perfect evenings, we'll have a delicious variety of Northwest regional foods prepared by the ship's expert cooks, including freshly caught crab, oysters, and salmon.

I'll tell your readers about the brewery tours, their premier beers, the gourmet meals, the schooner Zodiac, the guests, and the places we visit. I'll have lots of high-resolution photos to accompany this story.

This article will be of great interest to your readers because of its unique combination of Northwest beer, food, people, and places, plus the historic schooner. This piece will be

1500-1800 words and I'll be happy to write it to your specifications.

I'm a full time professional freelance travel writer with more than 250 articles published 450 times in over 130 regional, national and international magazines, newspapers, e-zines and In-flights. My beer stories have been published in Beers-of-the-World (Belgium's Top Ten Beer Festivals), Zymurgy (The Heavenly Brews of Belgium's Trappist Monasteries), and Beer & Brewer (Australia).

Other magazines and e-zines publishing my work include Scotland Magazine, Britain Magazine, Go World Travel, Tourist Travel, Travel Post Monthly, Northwest Travel, Columbia Gorge, Sunday Oregonian, 48 Degrees North, New Zealand Sunday News, Renaissance, Mysteries, Sculpture, and Open Skies In-flight magazines.

For clips of my work please go to my writer's website at www.Roy-Stevenson.com. Clips are also available upon request.

Thank you for consideration of this article. Please contact me at your earliest convenience if this piece looks like a good fit for your magazine. I look forward to hearing from you.

Best Regards,

Roy Stevenson

# CO-AUTHORING AND INTRIGUE: BEER MAGAZINE

This was one of my first breakthroughs into international travel magazines. I pitched this story to Beers-Of-The-World Magazine, which sadly is now defunct.

For one of my very early efforts, this is a good, solid query letter. It's cleanly written and paints a good picture of Belgian beer festivals. Note how the first three pitch paragraphs describe the beer festivals to give the editor a general feeling of their ambiance.

Also, note how we titillated the editor by stating that some of our choices of beer festivals would surprise her. We wanted to hook and intrigue her enough to buy our article. It worked!

Editors will usually go for something that presents an unusual view or perspective. Readers are always interested in something a little different.

The editor liked this piece enough to turn it into a cover story. I co-wrote this story with another writer who had expertise in the field. It's okay to do this, and it's a good way to start your writing career. Just make sure you get an agreement on who is doing what, and how you are going to share the payment. In this case, I did the sales pitch, we both worked on the article, and we split the payment down the middle.

To: Ms. <Editor's name>, Editor, Beers Of The World Magazine

Subject: Query re article "Belgium's Top Ten Beer Festivals".

Dear Ms. <Editor's name>,

We'd like to submit a piece telling Beers Of The World Magazine readers about "Belgium's Top Ten Beer Festivals". Every year hundreds of thousands of Belgian and foreign beer aficionados travel to dozens of small towns and several large cities in Belgium to participate in some of the finest beer festivals in the world.

These festivals range from subdued lowbrow tasting on medieval cobblestone squares in small stone villages in the Ardennes, with white tablecloths, to major extravaganzas where you're inside enormous white canvas tents or school gymnasiums, sitting at heavy wooden tables with well stained and worn surfaces, accordion and brass oompah music blaring in your ears.

Beer experts swirl, sniff, sip, and taste everything from dark potent heady Trappist beers to light subtly flavored summer ales, many taking copious notes after each sampling—this can be serious business. It's for good reason that Belgians rival the Germans as the world's leading connoisseurs of the frothy amber liquid. Belgian beer is an iconic symbol of beer quality around the world.

The article will be 1800-2300 words describing the top ten beer festivals in Belgium, their venues, a little about their host towns and cities, and what each festival is known for. There'll be an interesting mix of large and small town festivals, some world renown, some much smaller, but weighing in well above their size for quality--some of our choices will surprise you. We're sure you can guess five of our selections, but we bet you can't guess the rest of them. Our highly scientific rating system was based on three criteria: beer quality, beer quantity and fest atmosphere.

We'll list the dates for these events and describe the standard protocols for attending these festivals for first timers, from locating your obscure Belgian town (use a GPS or go by train from Brussels), to plunking down your euros for beer tokens and making sure you get your share of the ubiquitous cheese cubes sitting around the tables. We'll also describe a few of the special activities at these festivals; competitions and games that only someone with four or five monastic beers inside of him or her would attempt—often leading to some interesting spectacles and photographs that have the potential to destroy future political careers.

I'm a freelance writer with over 150 published articles on travel and culture, art, military history, film festival reviews, and fitness and health in over 50 different regional, national and international magazines, newspapers and e-zines. Clips or links are available upon request. We have some photographs of Belgian Beer festivals available.

I've just spent two years living in Brussels, Belgium. Having the luxury of not working during this time, I traveled constantly to dozens of small and large Belgian village, towns and cities, and got to know the Belgian psyche with all its foibles and big heartedness.

Joe Stange, the beer professional (and I mean professional--he's one of the guys taking notes at these festivals) is a career journalist and writer with dozens of Belgian beer festivals under his belt. He's our man in Brussels, in the trenches at these beer festivals.

This article will be of great interest to readers of Beers Of The World Magazine because it will show them what professionally organized Belgian beer festivals are really like, and hopefully motivate some of your readers to visit them.

Thank you for your consideration of this article. I look forward to hearing from you at your convenience.

Best Regards,

Roy Stevenson

# SHOW YOUR ENTHUSIASM: AUTOMOBILE MAGAZINE

This is yet another example of combining travel writing with another of my passions. Quite early in my freelance writing career I discovered that I enjoyed learning about classic and vintage automobiles. This began many enjoyable gigs with Collectible Automobile Magazine that continue to this day.

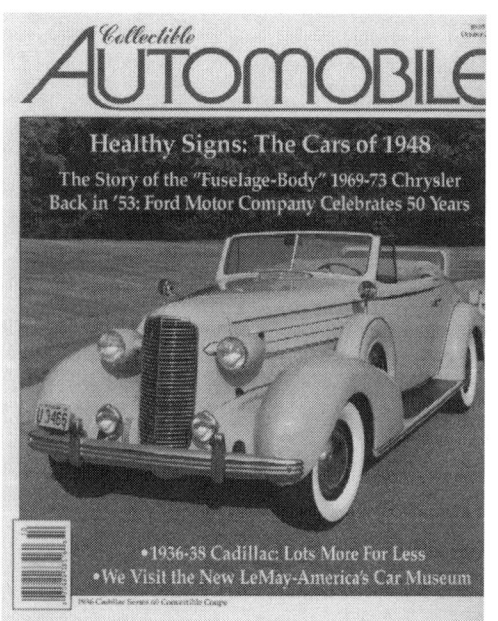

I'd written two articles for this magazine, and here is my pitch for my third article, about the LeMay America's Car Museum in Tacoma, Washington. I'd learned that the brand new LeMay Museum was just opening its doors, so thought I'd better pitch the Collectible Automobile Magazine editor before someone else beat me to it. This museum is less than an hour's drive from Seattle.

I already had a solid relationship with the editor. So I was able to dispense with the usual background information about my bylines. I simply reminded the editor about my previous two articles he'd published and then launched straight into my pitch.

This brings up a good point for beginners who are reading this eBook. If you've already had a story or three published in a magazine, don't assume that the editor remembers you. Chances are that he or she will, but it's wise to remind them of a couple of your previous published stories.

I did a lot of research about the new museum and it really shows in my query letter. I contacted the museum's media director well in advance and got on his press mailing list and newsletter distribution list, so I had access to lots of information. I make it clear to the magazine editor that I have already become an expert on this new museum, even though it hasn't yet opened to the public.

Also note that I show my flexibility about focusing on anything the editor prefers. The other thing that comes through loud and clear is my enthusiasm for the museum and the article. It's okay to show an editor that you're excited about a project. It makes an editor think: "Fresh blood, new ideas, great!"

Dear Mr. (Editor's name>,

I hope all is going well for you. Roy Stevenson here. I have previously submitted two articles to Classic Automobile (WAAAM Museum at Hood River, and National Motor Museum, England).

I am wondering if I can interest you in a piece about the LeMay America's Car Museum that is under construction in Tacoma, Washington? The website is www.lemaymuseum.org. I live 50 minutes away from the museum site.

This museum is going to be nothing short of fantastic! This will be, from what I have seen, a world-class shrine to the automobile. It will be a center of car culture, and I imagine it will very quickly become one of the most famous automobile museums in the world.

I have recently visited with the museum's marketing officer, Scot Keller, and he has shared the plans with me. The museum is due to open on May 19, 2012, and will be 165,000 square feet. It will be massive. A scan through the museum's website gives good insight into the enormity of this center.

The museum will feature a 3.5-acre grass show field, and over 400 automobiles rotating in from a total collection of 1900. It will be the largest privately held automobile museum in the world, and second largest after the Peterson Collection in Nevada.

The museum will be an education center to promote automotive history, restoration and preservation, and a place where enthusiasts from around the world will come to celebrate automobiles. It will feature a vintage car concourse and drive in movies that will play on the outside wall of the museum.

My proposed article will cover the new museum, its purposes, and of course the automobiles displayed there. I'm happy to include anything else that you need to be covered. As this museum is not due to be completed until May of next year, I would simply like to get your commitment to this story in advance, and then present the story to you after the opening date.

Please let me know of your interest, and if this will be a good fit for the magazine.

Best Regards,

Roy Stevenson

# BUILD LONG-TERM RELATIONSHIPS: MILITARY MAGAZINE

Way back when I started freelance writing, I was already passionately interested in military topics that involved travel. I wanted to write about military museums, vehicles, forts, battlefields, and cemeteries. This eventually expanded into writing about antique military weapons and artillery.

This pitch landed me my first article in Military Machines International, a popular U.K. military vehicle publication. Believe it or not, there are several military vehicle magazines published around the world!

The story I pitched was about military vehicles at Fort Lewis, Washington, and marked the beginning of a beautiful relationship with this magazine.

The pitch section of this query letter is five paragraphs long, and provides a lot of detail about the topic. I had done a lot of research about Fort Lewis, and it shows in this letter. Notice that I offer photographs to accompany this article. I also mention that I'll supply some quotes from the museum curator, a good practice to get into. Quotes really break up a story and inject some life into it.

Seven years later, I still get my military vehicle museum stories published in this magazine.

Since this article was published, I've had assignments to write about military museums, forts, and battlefields around the world including:

France (Normandy, Paris); Luxembourg (Diekirk); Germany (Berlin, Karlshorst, Gatow, Spandau, Aachen, Dachau, Nuremberg, Munich); the Netherlands (Best, Overloon); the U.S.A. (Fort Lewis, Washington, Long Beach, Virginia, Tucson, Arizona, Ketchikan, Nebraska, Chicago, Portland, Oregon, Texas, Missouri, Florida); England (London, Woolwich, Portsmouth, Dover, Fort Nelson, Leeds, Duxford, Bovington, Kent, Bletchley Park, Norwich); Belgium (Brussels, Waterloo, Bastogne, Ardennes-Poteau, Eben-Emael); Scotland (Edinburgh Castle); Finland (Helsinki Sveaborg Fortress, Parola); Hungary (Budapest); and others. You get the idea.

Imagine - getting paid to visit places you've always wanted to visit!

TO: Mr. <Editor's Name>, Editor, Military Machines International.

Subject: Query re article "The Military Vehicles at Fort Lewis Military Museum, Tacoma, Washington".

Dear Mr. <Editor's name>,

I'd like to submit a piece telling Military Machines International readers about "The Military Vehicles at Fort Lewis Military Museum, Tacoma, Washington".

The enormous 86,000-acre, 120,000-person, Fort Lewis U.S. Military Base sits astride busy Interstate 5 in Tacoma, a 45-minute drive south of Seattle, Washington. A stone's throw from the Interstate is the Fort Lewis Military Museum. You can just glimpse all sorts of military vehicles and tanks standing around outside, as you zip past an interesting looking, old, white wooden building.

There are a variety of military vehicles—22 in all, dating from World War Two to the present, displayed outside in the vehicle park. A few stand under a long open-sided shelter you can walk through. All are in an excellent state of preservation. They range from World War Two vintage like the proverbial M4A1 Sherman tank, an M3A1 Stuart light tank, an M24 Chaffee light tank, to the Patton tank (1962), and the M103A1 Heavy tank. More exotic light vehicles like the XR 311 Experimental High Mobility Vehicle (aka "Dune Buggy") of 1970, to the Experimental Fast Attack Vehicle now used by Navy SEALS in Operation Desert Storm are also displayed.

There are half-tracks, APCs, and even a few missiles strewn around the vehicle park—a Nike-Hercules missile, and an Honest John Rocket. And a few battle acquisitions such as the Chinese Type 59 tank. Mobile artillery guns and anti-aircraft guns round out an exciting display.

I'd like to tell Military Machines International readers about the military vehicles, the museum contents, the (brief) history surrounding the museum building, and a little about Fort Lewis. I have some good quotes from the museum curator, John Archambault, and I'll provide directions for the visitor and instructions on how guests and visitors can enter the fort—you can't just drive in.

I have a selection of 46 great photos of the military vehicles, and plenty more photos of the exhibits inside the museum.

The article will be 1300-1500 words and will be a good addition to your occasional overseas military vehicle museum coverage, all the more interesting because it's on a working military base.

I'm a freelance writer with over 170 articles published on military history, history, travel and culture, film festival reviews and fitness in over 50 different regional, national and international magazines, newspapers and ezines. My work covering military topics has appeared in Classic Military Vehicle, Militaria International, Military, Army Motor, Airborne Quarterly, Static Line, Monitoring Times and Popular Communications. Clips are available on request.

Thank you for considering this article. I look forward to hearing from you at your convenience.


Best Regards,

Roy Stevenson

# "DEAR EDITOR" QUERY: SPECIALTY MAGAZINE

Here's another example of how I have pitched a specialty magazine with what is, essentially, a travel story.

I'd always wanted to see this fun UFO Festival in McMinnville, Oregon, so what better way to see the event and get paid for it, than to pitch the story to a UFO magazine? The editor jumped on the article (and several others since) and I had a blast at this event.

Note that I addressed the query letter to "The Editor". This isn't normally an acceptable practice because we don't want to offend the editor. Also, an editor may think you're a lazy writer if you can't be bothered to find his name. In this case, I tried my best to find the editor's name, but simply couldn't locate it anywhere, so I wrote this generic greeting.

My personal opinion is that if you have a good enough pitch, an editor will overlook normal protocols and go with your story idea.

I certainly don't recommend this approach because it's risky, and I'm all about reducing risk of rejection by editors. Nevertheless, I have to tell you that I've had a number of published articles resulting from query letters where I wrote "Dear Editor". Do your best to find a name, but when you can't find it, send the query anyway.

My pitch is four paragraphs long—about normal for my query letters. It's an enticing query and I'm trying to sow the idea in the editor's mind that the story will be lively and interesting by using those actual terms in the first sentence. Whether this was good journalism is open for debate, but I did sell the story.

You'll also notice that I spell out very clearly in the fourth paragraph exactly what my story will be about. I'm really big on this, and you'll see this recurring throughout my query letters. I try to write a clear statement in all of my query letters, and it significantly improves my chances of getting the story into print.

To: The Editor, Open Minds Magazine

Subject: Query re article, "Aliens on the Streets: The McMinnville UFO Festival",

Dear Editor,

If you're looking for an offbeat, lively and interesting UFO story, I'd like to offer an article about the second largest gathering of UFO aficionados in the United States. The Annual UFO Festival in McMinnville, Oregon, now in its eleventh year, celebrates a well documented UFO sighting in 1950 by a local farmer, who took several photographs of the object that are still unchallenged by experts today.

This event occurs in mid-May and consists of a varied schedule of events from the serious to the ridiculous. Several of the world's most renown UFOlogists including Stanton Friedman, Linda Moulton Howe, and Peter Davenport (Director of the National UFO Reporting Center) have presented on a variety of topics including abductions and recent and famous UFO cases.

Eyewitnesses have described their dramatic sightings, and experts have spoken about crop circles. UFO films are shown in the evenings. On the wackier side, there's a spectacular UFO Costume Parade along McMinnville's Main Street, an Alien Pet Costume Contest, and an Alien Costume Ball.

I'd like to tell your readers about this UFO festival, the speakers, attendees, and events that make it one of the U.S.A.'s most renowned UFO gatherings.

I anticipate this piece will be 1200-1500 words but I'll be happy to size it to your specifications. I will have many high-resolution photos to accompany this article.

I'm a full time professional freelance travel writer with more than 350 articles appearing in over 150 regional, national and international magazines, newspapers, websites and In-flights. My articles on the paranormal and UFOs have been published in Mysteries Magazine, www.ufos-aliens.co.uk, www.ufocasebook.com, and www.ufosnw.com.

For samples of my writing please go to my writer's website at www.Roy-Stevenson.com. Magazines publishing my work include *Britain Magazine, Scotland Magazine, Renaissance,*

*Zymurgy, Sculpture, Open Skies In-flight, Go World Travel, Tourist Travel, Travellady, Travel Post Monthly, Mid-Columbian, Northwest Travel, South Sound, Columbia Gorge, Kitsap Sun, Sunday Oregonian, 48 Degrees North,* and *Colors Northwest.*

Thank you for your consideration of this article. Please contact me if this piece looks like a good fit your magazine. I look forward to hearing from you at your convenience.

 Best Regards,

Roy Stevenson

# REPACKAGING AND REPURPOSING YOUR STORIES: YACHTING MAGAZINE

I've been writing Puget Sound Marina destination travel articles for a regional yachting magazine for several years. I wrote so many marina articles that I finally ran out of marinas!

What to do? Repackage. It's something every freelance travel writer can do when you have several articles on a specific topic.

By repackaging my marina destination stories I was able to sell them to other sailing magazines.

I repurposed some of my Puget Sound marina articles, repackaged them for the Canadian audience, and resold them to a Canadian Yachting magazine.

In this query letter I point out why the magazine's readers will find my proposed story interesting. Many Canadians sail down into U.S. waters every summer, and my marina descriptions will help them choose which ones to visit.

Notice the paragraph where I list my by-lines. The order of publications is important. I'm careful to lead off with three yachting magazines followed by the regional travel magazines where I've been published. Together, these establish my bona fides nicely. And this short 3-paragraph pitch didn't take very long to write.

To: Mr. <Editor's name>, Editor, Canadian Yachting West

Subject: Query re article, "The Top Ten Marina Destinations in the Puget Sound".

Dear Mr. <Editor's name>,

I'd like to submit a piece telling your readers about "The Top Ten Marina Destinations in the Puget Sound".

The article will cover Roche Harbor, Port Ludlow, Friday Harbor, Langley, Port Gamble, Olympia, Thea Foss Waterway (Tacoma), Anacortes, Deer Harbor, Bellingham (Squalicum Harbor), and/or Port Orchard. The article will include mooring details at these marinas, restaurants popular with sailors, and nearby attractions.

This article will be of great interest to your readers because the Puget Sound is one of the world's finest marina destination places and many Canadians sail down and spend weeks and even all summer there.

I anticipate this piece will be 1500 words but I'll be happy to write it to your specifications. I have plenty of high-resolution photos to accompany this article.

I'm a full time professional freelance travel writer and photographer with more than 700 articles published in 170 regional, national, and international magazines, newspapers, online travel magazines and in-flights. I'm considered to be one of the most prolific freelance writers in the U.S.A.

My work has appeared in *Classic Boat, Blue Water Sailing, 48 Degrees North, Northwest Travel, South Sound, Columbia Gorge, Off-road Adventures, Scotland Magazine, Britain Magazine, This England, Australia & New Zealand, Sunday Oregonian, New Zealand Sunday News, Emirates Open Skies In-flight, Beers-of-the-World, Beer Connoisseur, Cheese Connoisseur, Coast Food & Arts, Sculpture, Lost Treasure, Northwest Meetings & Events, World War II Quarterly, Mid-Columbian Zymurgy, Mysteries, Kitsap Sun, GoNomad.com, YourLifeIsATrip.com, GoWorldTravel.com, TouristTravel.com, Travellady.com, TravelPostMonthly.com, Travelmag.co.uk,*, and many other publications.

For clips of my work please go to my writer's website at www.Roy-Stevenson.com. Please also take a moment to look at the Editor's Comments section on my website. PDF clips are also available upon request.

Thank you for consideration of this article. Please contact me if this piece looks like a good fit for your magazine. I look forward to hearing from you at your convenience.

Best Regards,

Roy Stevenson

# USE AVAILABLE CONTENT IN YOUR QUERY: CRUISE MAGAZINE

This query resulted in an article about Petersburg, Alaska, published in Compass Magazine, the On-board magazine for Holland America Cruise Line. I had already written the story, so didn't hesitate to lift out large chunks and use them in this lengthy query letter.

If you have some good written material already available, use it!

This query letter is the standard format I use today. My lead off sentence states the story title, and then I use a few paragraphs to elaborate about the place I'm pitching.

Then I offer a gallery of high res photographs with the story to sweeten the pot. Finally, I cap off a nice query by listing some of my bylines and directing the editor to have a look at my writer's website for samples of my writing.

This query also refers the editor to my writer's website section called "Editors Comments" which consists of endorsements from editors that I have worked for in the past. Instant references when working with a new editor!

To: Mr. <Editor's name>

Subject: Query re article, "Petersburg, Alaska's little Norway: Millionaire Fishermen, a Magnificent Glacier and Magical Muskeg Swamp"

Dear Mr. <Editor's Name>,

I'd like to submit a piece telling your readers about my recent experiences in Petersburg, Alaska.

I disembarked from the Alaska Marine Highway ferry at the Petersburg dock with some trepidation. Due to spend five days in this small Alaskan fishing town of only 3,030 inhabitants, my stay could have been a boring eternity. After all, Petersburg is not Petersburg—if you know what I mean.

I needn't have worried—Mitkof Island's multitude of offerings swept me off my feet in a pleasant, low-key way. My dance card was packed solid: I toured a massive ice-blue glacier (twice—I enjoyed it so much I went back for a second visit!), paddled between huge icebergs the size of houses in a misty sound with deer ambling along the shoreline, and hiked through a mysterious Muskeg swamp.

I learned about the town's storied Norwegian heritage at the local Sons of Norway Hall and the Clausen Memorial museum, and explored ancient Native American Tlingit fish traps on a rocky beach. Nearby, I puzzled over petroglyphs carved into a nearby rock two thousand years ago by the First People.

Other experiences took me into the heart of Petersburg life, like sitting in Kito's Kave, a dimly lit bar/restaurant/liquor store. Here, I discussed the stock market and the escalating price of halibut with leather skinned, flannel-shirted fishermen wearing brown Xtra-Tuff Gumboots while they cracked away on the pool table. My tour of a cannery, watching two-feet long King salmon being tossed around like flying fish showed me first hand the currency that makes this town go around. And by the end of my stay, many of the locals knew me, waved, and asked about my trip back to Seattle. It's that sort of place.

The busy little township of Petersburg, measuring six blocks by five blocks is friendly and welcoming; its residents genuinely impressed that visitors choose to visit. It's a working fishing town, and that's what they do here. Early in the morning the fishing boats glide gently out of the marina every few minutes, their crews filled with hope that they'll strike a big school of salmon—you can read the excitement on their faces.

Then, in the evenings, after the fishing boats come chugging in loaded to the gunnels with masses of struggling salmon in their deep holds, the fisherman and deck hands visit the local bars, their day's work done. Everyone has a surprisingly global perspective, more than you'd expect for a remote island in S.E. Alaska.

My article will show what Petersburg offered me. This article will be of great interest to your readers because Petersburg is off the beaten tourist track, and has plenty to offer.

This piece will be 1000 words and I will have plenty of high-resolution photos to accompany this article.

I'm a full time professional freelance travel writer and photographer with more than 700 articles published in 160 regional, national, and international magazines, newspapers, online travel magazines and in-flights. I am one of the most prolific freelance writers in the U.S.

My work has appeared in *Scotland Magazine, Britain Magazine, This England, Australia & New Zealand, Renaissance, Sunday Oregonian, New Zealand Sunday News, Emirates Open Skies In-flight, Beers-of-the-World, Beer Connoisseur, Blue Water Sailing, Cheese Connoisseur, Classic Boat, Coast Food & Arts, Sculpture, Lost Treasure, Northwest Meetings & Events, Popular Communications, World War II Quarterly, Mid-Columbian, Northwest Travel, South Sound, Columbia Gorge, Off-road Adventures, Zymurgy, Mysteries, Kitsap Sun, GoNomad.com, Go World Travel, Tourist Travel, Travellady, Travel Post Monthly, Travelmag.com*, and many other publications.

For clips of my work please go to my writer's website at www.Roy-Stevenson.com. Please also take a moment to look at the Editor's Comments section on my website.

Thank you for consideration of this article. I look forward to hearing from you at your convenience.

Best Regards,

Roy Stevenson

# PROVIDE HIGH QUALITY PHOTOS: MILITARY MAGAZINE

I had already submitted several short military museum stories to this editor, and was on a first name basis with him. My goal was to write a feature article for this highly regarded World War II magazine that included both a historical perspective and a travel description of what you can see today at this battle site.

I pitched the story idea in a stripped down query letter, as I had already established a rapport with the editor and he knew my military writing background.

This query letter helped me to achieve my goal. The editor ran the 6,000-word story and it helped pave the way for other World War II feature history/travel stories in other top shelf magazines in this genre.

This stripped down pitch is short and to the point, and was all that the editor needed to make up his mind.

Note that I offer a number of photographs to accompany the story. You'll notice this is a recurring sentence in my query letters. Offering photos to accompany a travel article often tips the scales in your favor and helps the editor make a decision.

The fact that you can provide images saves the editor a lot of time and effort. Don't underestimate the power of doing your own photography in today's freelance writing world.

These days my wife, who is a professional travel photographer, does most of the photos for my articles. But I have my own dSLR camera and can shoot some high-quality photos when I need to. Selling some of my photos along with articles has paid for the cost of my camera and lens several times over, not to mention have clinched the deal countless times.

If you're serious about travel writing, get a decent dSLR camera and learn the basics on how to take good quality, high resolution shots. Ask a photographer friend to help you choose the right camera if you're unsure about what to purchase.

Hi <Editor's name>,

Here's my story idea. Hope it will be a good fit for the magazine.

The fall of Belgium's Fort Eben Emael—Key to the Invasion of the Low Countries.

On May 11, 1940, seventy German paratroopers landed in gliders atop a Belgian fortress that was considered unassailable. It was nothing short of a suicide attack. Yet in less than an hour, this underground fortress, thought to be the most advanced fortress in Belgium's line of fortress defenses, was conquered and its 1,000 soldiers were defeated and marched off into captivity.

This was the first classic coup de main use of gliders in World War II, and proved a stunning success, with little loss of life on the Germans' part.

I'd like to tell the story of this battle and about the building and unsuccessful defense of Fort Eben Emael, and what it looks like today. I've visited the fort, inside and on top (where the gliders landed) and have 50 high res photos to accompany this story.

Best Regards,

Roy Stevenson

# TWEAKING YOUR TEMPLATE: TOP SHELF MAGAZINE

Smithsonian Air and Space Magazine is a top shelf magazine, and pays $1/word. You know you're doing something right when magazines like this accept your articles for publication.

This article was aimed at the military magazine market, a field in which I have been very successful in placing my stories, as you will see from my bylines in this query letter.

Note that I provide plenty of examples of military publications in my query, and go heavy on the technical details about the Flying Jeep. But the pitch is still only three paragraphs.

I believe in using templates for all repetitive tasks in order to be more productive. I've talked about this quite a bit on my website in an article about increasing your productivity. But it's important to know when to tweak your templates to suit a particular topic or genre. (http://www.pitchtravelwrite.com/increase-productivity-create-more-time.html.)

My query letters always starts out the same: "I'd like to submit a piece telling your readers about . . ."

And I always finish with the same three sentences, "Thank you for consideration of this article. Please contact me if this piece looks like a good fit for your magazine. I look forward to hearing from you at your convenience."

Bylines are tweaked to suit the genre and the particular publication keeping in mind what will get the attention of the editor.

Selling the story to the editor is by far the most important part of the query letter – so create your own template, save valuable time and spend your energy on the part that matters – pitching your story idea.

To: Ms. <Editor's name>, Editor, Air & Space Magazine

Subject: Query re article, "U.S. Army Aviation Vehicle Oddities That Never Made Production"

Dear Ms. <Editor's name>,

I'd like to submit a piece telling your readers about unusual aviation vehicles developed and tested by the U.S. Army that were never commissioned for production.

I came across the prototypes of these machines while visiting the U.S. Army Transport Museum at Fort Eustis, Virginia recently. These vehicles all "worked"; they flew or hovered successfully, and did what they were designed to do. But they never made it to the assembly line for one reason or another, and seem today to be the stuff of science fiction.

Here's a brief bio of the aviation vehicles.

Piaseki developed the "Flying Jeep" under contract with the transportation Research and experimental Command at Fort Eustis. The initial model, the VZ8P-1 first flew in May 1958, and is exhibited at the American Helicopter Museum in West Chester, PA.

The second Flying Jeep model, at the U.S. Army Transport Museum, the VZ8P-2, was also built by Mr. Piaseki. He improved the initial design by placing the rear rotor at a slant, providing forward thrust. The Jeep first flew at Piasecki's Philadelphia plant in December 1962.

Both models were powered by the three-blade rotors and two Artouste II turbine engines, which generated lift. All major components were housed in the chassis, thereby reducing hazards of conventional helicopters to personnel on the ground.

This article will be of great interest to your readers because few people know about these unique aviation vehicles and their development.

I anticipate this piece will be 1200-1500 words but I'll be happy to write it to your specifications. I have several high-resolution photos of each of these vehicles, and have access to more via the museum's curator.

I'm a freelance writer based in Seattle, Washington, specializing in military vehicles and aviation, military museums, memorials and cemeteries, military history, fortifications, artillery, weapons, and signals and communications. To see samples of my military articles please go to http://www.roy-stevenson.com/roy-stevenson-military-history.html.

I have more than 125 military articles published in the U.S., U.K., Scotland and New Zealand, and 800 freelance travel articles in 180 magazines, newspapers, and in-flights and online travel magazines. I write the monthly military museum column for *Military Magazine* (U.S.) and *Classic Arms & Militaria* (U.K.).

My military articles have appeared in *World War II Quarterly, Armchair General, Warbird Digest, Aviation History, Army Motors, Classic Military Vehicle (UK), Military Machines International (UK), Classic Arms & Militaria (UK), The Artilleryman, Military Magazine, Scale Military Modeller International (UK), Strategy & Tactics, SpaceFlight (UK), Airborne Quarterly, Off-Road Adventures, Jeep Action, Renaissance, Scotland, Sunday Oregonian, Monitoring Times, Popular Communications, South Sound, New Zealand Sunday News,* and *Kitsap Sun.*

For general clips of my work please go to my writer's website at www.Roy-Stevenson.com. Please also take a moment to look at the Editor's Comments section on my website.

Thank you for consideration of this article. Please contact me if this piece looks like a good fit for your magazine. I look forward to hearing from you at your convenience.

Best Regards,

Roy Stevenson

# BEYOND THE QUERY LETTER
# MARKETING MASTERY FORMULA™

When I talk with aspiring freelance writers at writer's conferences, they often tell me that they have plenty of story ideas but they never get to actually market their articles because something always seems to hold them back from unleashing their inner marketing juggernaut. Marketing tends to stop a lot of people dead in their tracks.

As a beginning freelance writer, what would you think if you suddenly pitched several stories and had most of them accepted for publication? Yikes! You'd actually have to sit down and write the articles.

This is the "problem" that I face daily—I always have stories to write and deadlines to meet—a problem that freelance writers love to have.

I believe my high acceptance "hit" rate by magazine editors comes from doing a number of things thoroughly rather than just doing one thing.

**In fact, there is a series of things you must do to boost your chances of convincing editors that your article will be a good fit in their magazine. And every one of these things must be done well. I call this my Marketing Mastery Formula™.**

My **Marketing Mastery Formula™** uses this principle and includes six core activities:

1. Dreaming up a saleable topic idea.
2. Researching your topic thoroughly.

3. Finding and researching publications to pitch your idea.
4. Creating a query letter that resonates with the editor.
5. Delivering a quality article on time.
6. Getting repeat business with that editor.

I call this my **Marketing Mastery Formula™** because it consists of six core activities. These six core activities are like a chain and must all be performed well. You can't have a weak link. If a chain has a weak link, it will break at that link when it is stressed.

**Mastering all six activities ensures a strong foundation for success.**

If there is a deficiency in the preparation and presentation of your story query, for example, an experienced editor will notice it, and your chances of getting the piece accepted for publication will decrease significantly.

You can fail at any one of these six core activities and that will impact your ability to be successful. If you neglect any one of the core links in this chain, your chances of being published plummet. I address these six core activities, my **Marketing Mastery Formula™** in my book *"The Complete Guide to Selling and Marketing Your Travel Articles"*.

Whatever your motivation for wanting to write and be published, you should know it's never been easier. You can send out a query email and receive an acceptance email back from the editor within an hour. (My record is ten minutes from pitch to acceptance). Then you email the article back within a couple of days and see your story in print a few months later. It's as close as you can get to instant gratification.

My manual includes my best advice on how to market your story pitches maximally, get your stories into print and get paid.

You can find more information on the Writer's Resources page of this book.

# WRITER'S RESOURCES

**100 Print Magazines that Want to Publish Your Travel Articles** is a list of 100 print magazines that publish articles from freelance writers. It's the list I use to sell my travel articles. This list will save you hundreds of hours of time - time you can spend writing and traveling instead! It's also packed with expert advice to help you get published more often.
http://www.pitchtravelwrite.com/print-magazines.html

**50 Websites that Want to Publish Your Travel Articles** is a list of 50+ quality websites along with ten pages of advice about getting published online. Save yourself hundreds of hours of research time with this list of websites at your fingertips every time you want to get one of your stories published.
http://www.pitchtravelwrite.com/fifty-websites.html

**How to Land Press Trips and Fam Tours** will show you how to use your travel writing skills and credentials so you can request free or discounted travel, meals, tours, accommodations and entry into museums and tourist attractions. If you want to land more press trips, you will find valuable resources to help you do that in this 75-page, comprehensive guide.
http://www.pitchtravelwrite.com/how-to-land-press-trips.html

**How to Break Into the Luxury Travel Writing Market** will put you on the fast track for success with luxury travel writing. If you enjoy staying at luxury resorts, villas and spas, enjoy eating at the finest restaurants and being treated like royalty, this 130-page eBook will help you learn how to do this. Step-by-step instructions tell you exactly what you need to know to succeed in this niche.

http://www.pitchtravelwrite.com/luxury-travel-writing-ebook.html

**The Complete Guide to Marketing & Selling Your Travel Articles** explains all the marketing techniques I use to sell articles. It's my complete system from dreaming up salable story ideas and creating enticing query letters to selling your articles successfully. If you follow the advice in this manual, it will radically shorten your learning curve for freelance writing success.

http://www.pitchtravelwrite.com/marketing-and-selling-your-travel-articles-ebook.html

**www.PitchTravelWrite.com** - a very popular website created for freelance travel writers. PitchTravelWrite.com is full of free content about how to sell your travel stories, the travel writing craft, and travel topics. Sign up for the free weekly eZine with marketing tips, writing advice and other valuable topics at: http://www.pitchtravelwrite.com/pitchtravelwrite-ezine.html.

# ABOUT THE AUTHOR

Roy Stevenson is a professional freelance travel writer and photographer, specializing in a wide variety of genres. These include travel and culture, historical travel, military history, food, beer and wine, classic cars, sailing, communications, film festivals, running and triathlon training, fitness, health, and other topics that interest him.

Since he started freelance writing in 2007, Stevenson has had more than 900 articles published in regional, national, and international media. His work has appeared in over 190 magazines, in-flights, on-boards, newspapers, trade journals, and online travel websites around the world. His articles have been in magazines in major bookstores continuously since December 2007. You can find a selection of published articles on his professional writing website www.roy-stevenson.com.

Many writing magazines have featured Stevenson's "how-to" articles including Writer's News, The New Writer, The Writer, Writer's Weekly.com, and he contributes frequently to Writer's Forum Magazine. He also speaks at various writer's conferences every year.

Roy is also the author of a very popular website created for freelance travel writers. www.PitchTravelWrite.com is full of free content about how to sell your travel stories, the travel writing craft, and other travel writing topics. He publishes a weekly e-Zine with marketing tips and writing advice. You can sign up at http://www.pitchtravelwrite.com/pitchtravelwrite-ezine.html.

Manufactured by Amazon.ca
Bolton, ON

28657406R00063